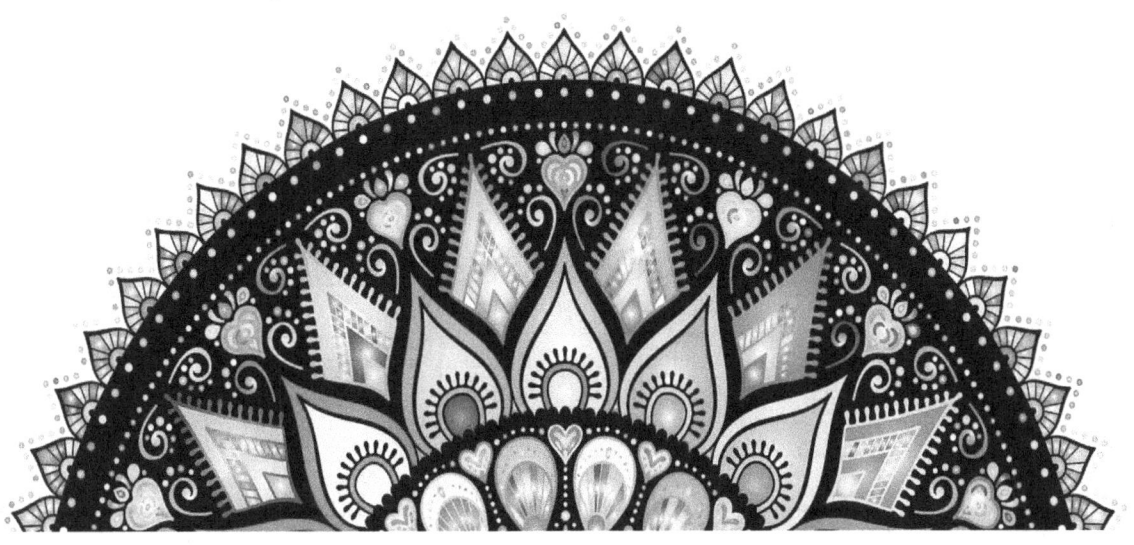

Dieses Malbuch gehört zu :

....

....

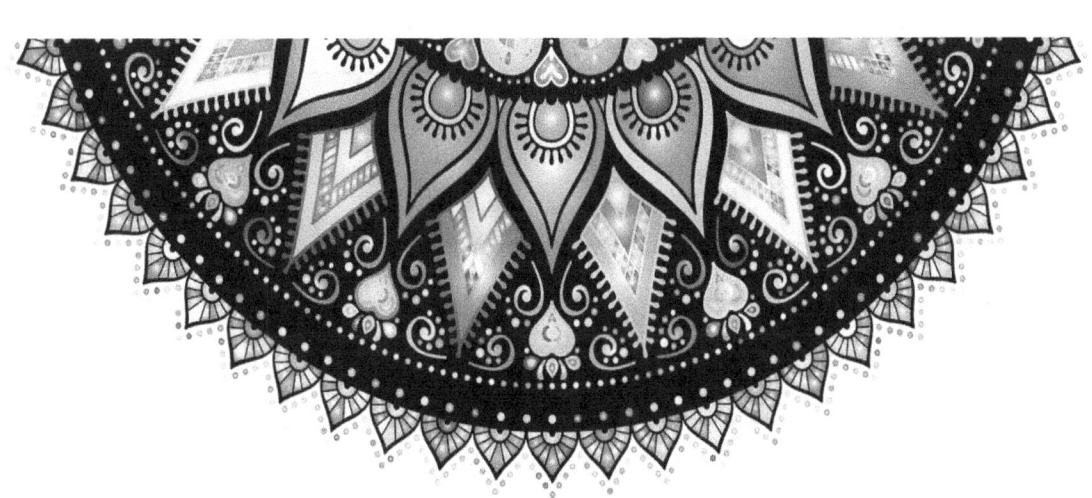

SEITENFARB TEST

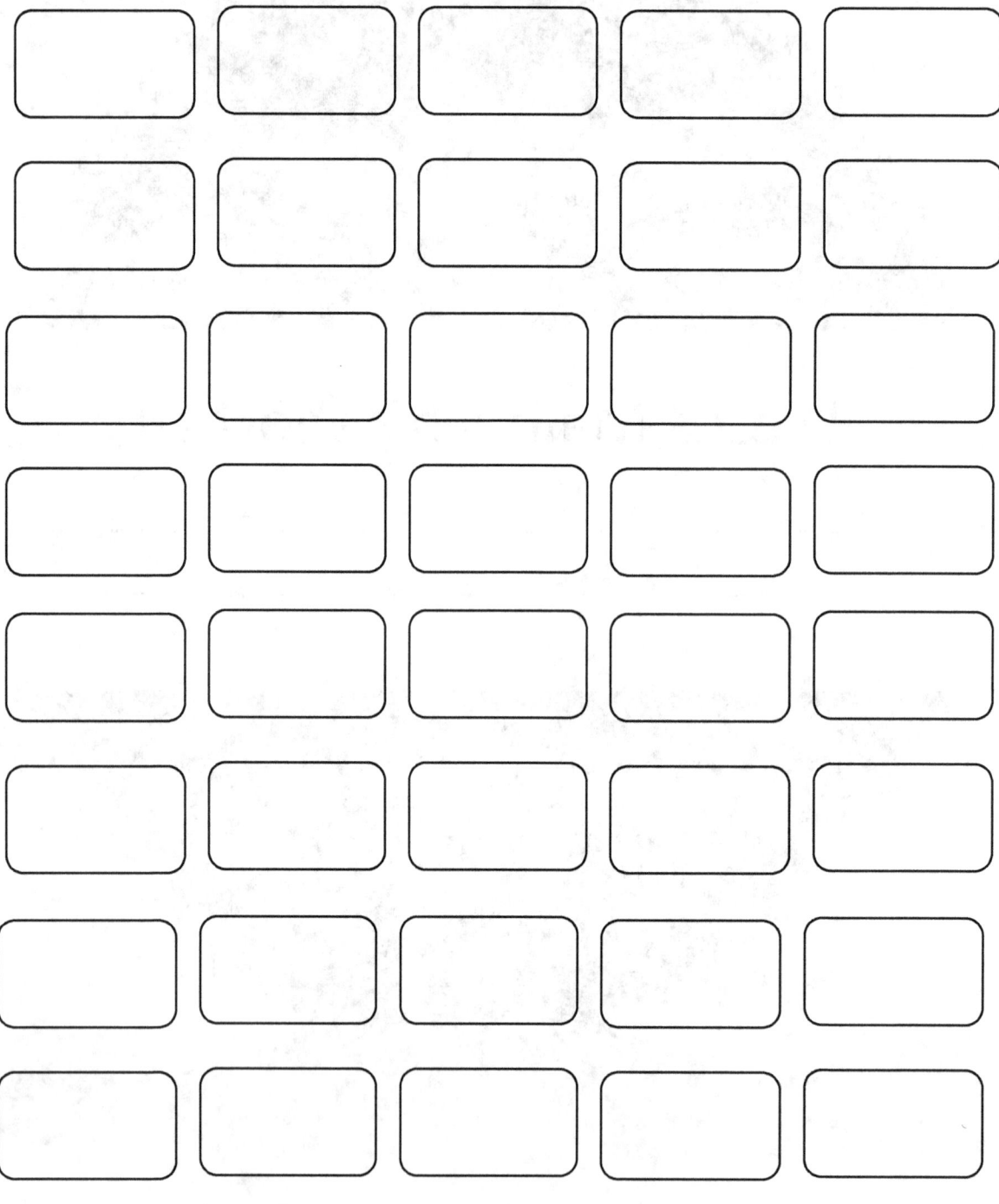

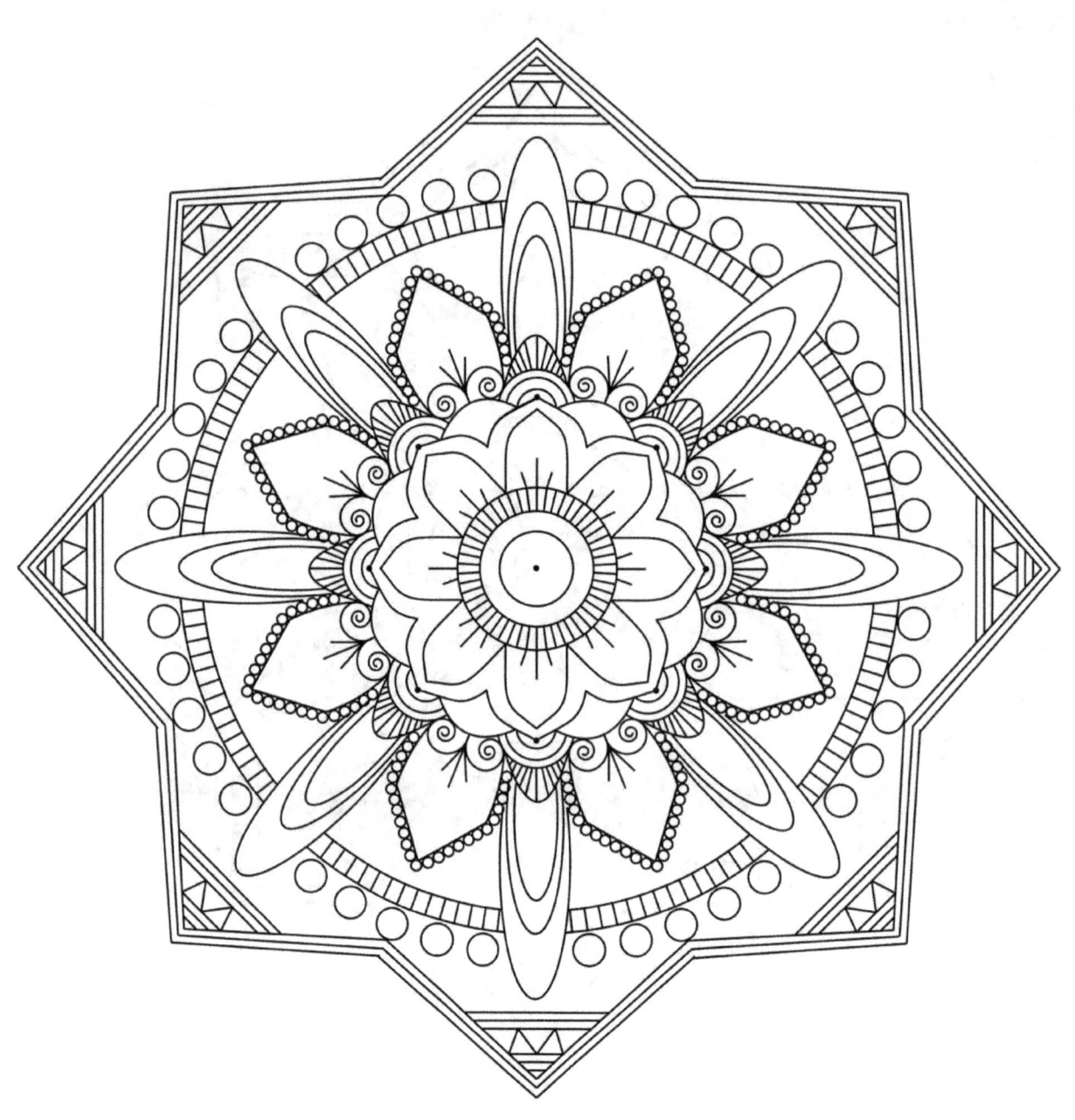

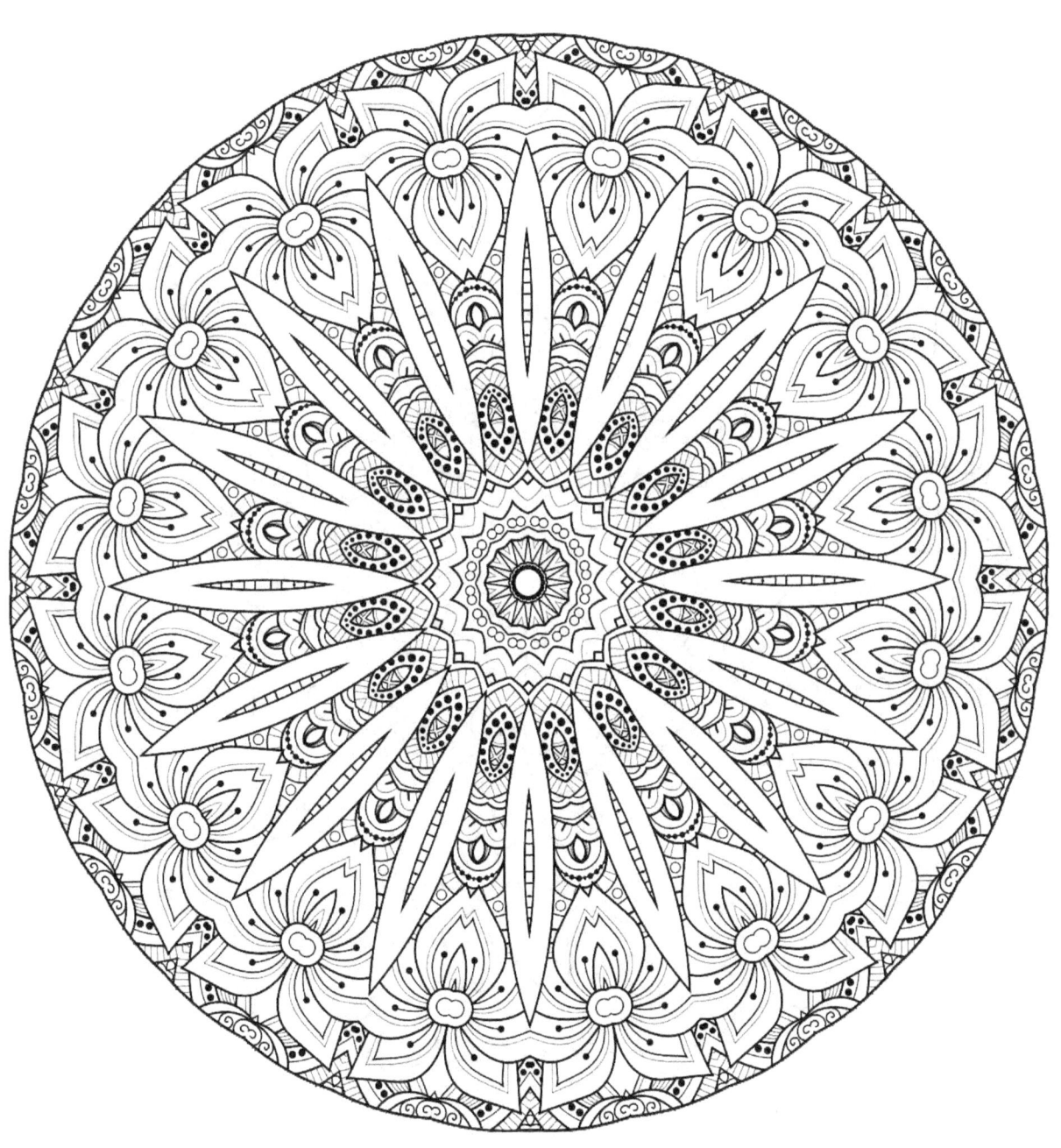

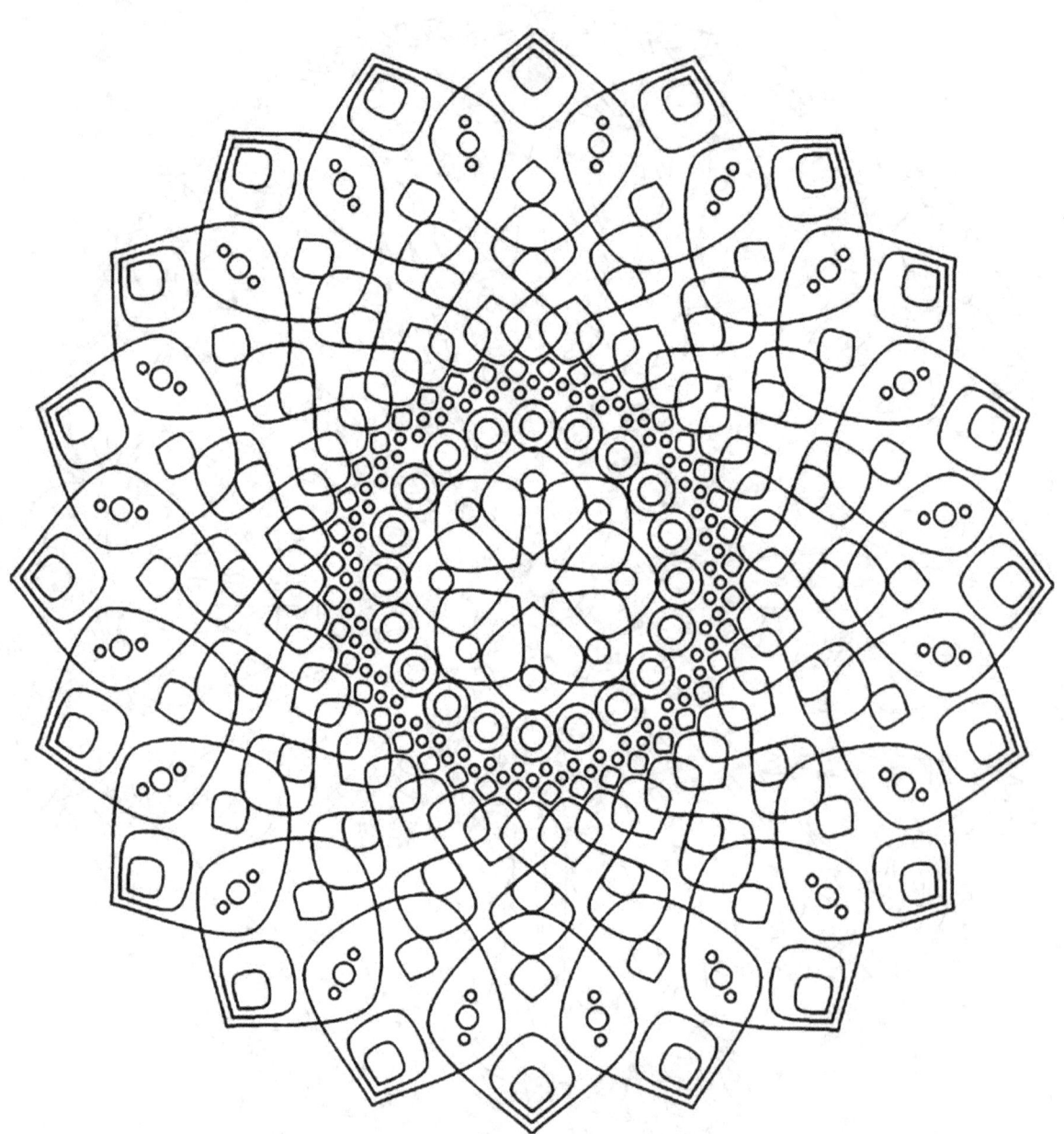

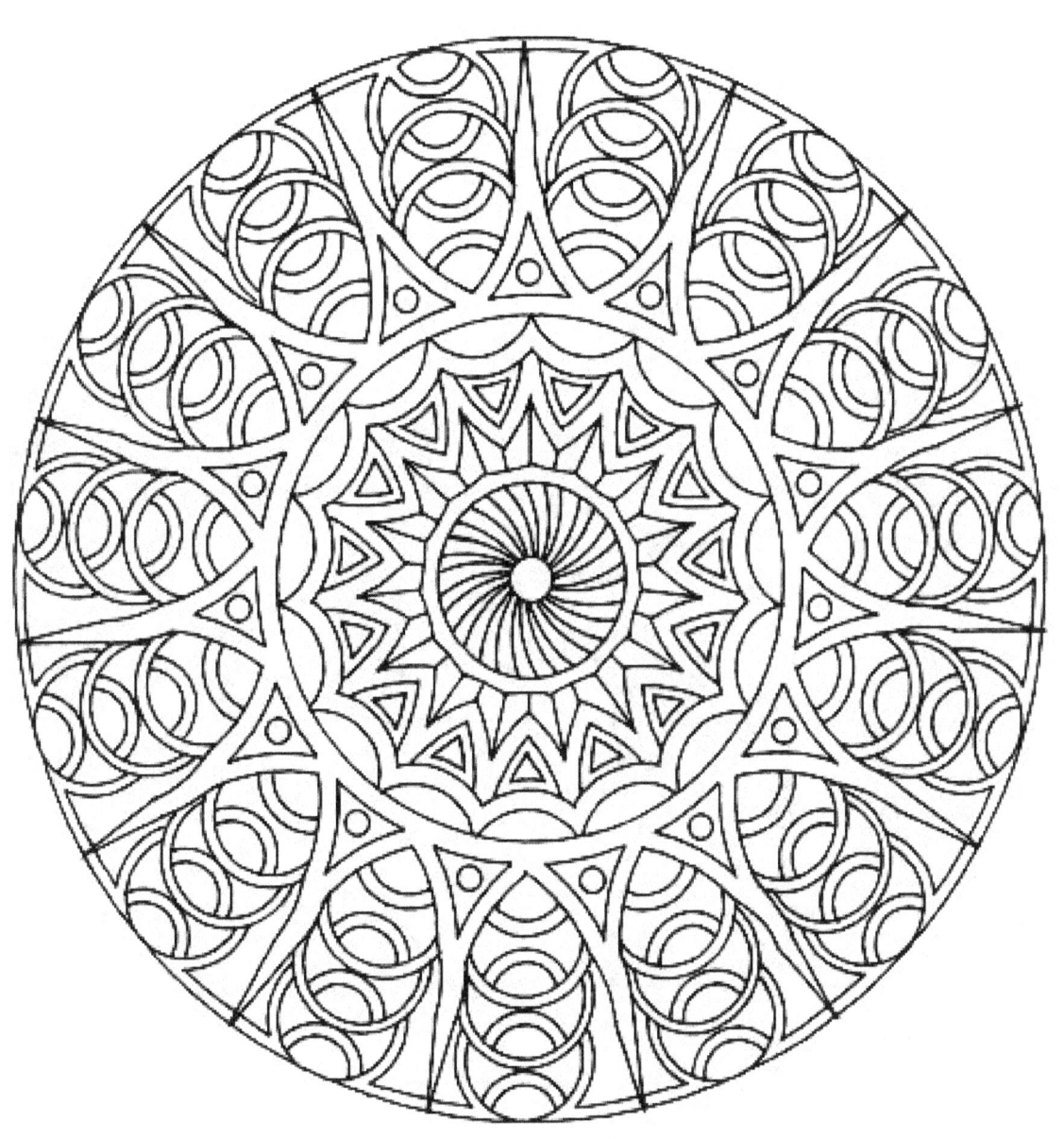

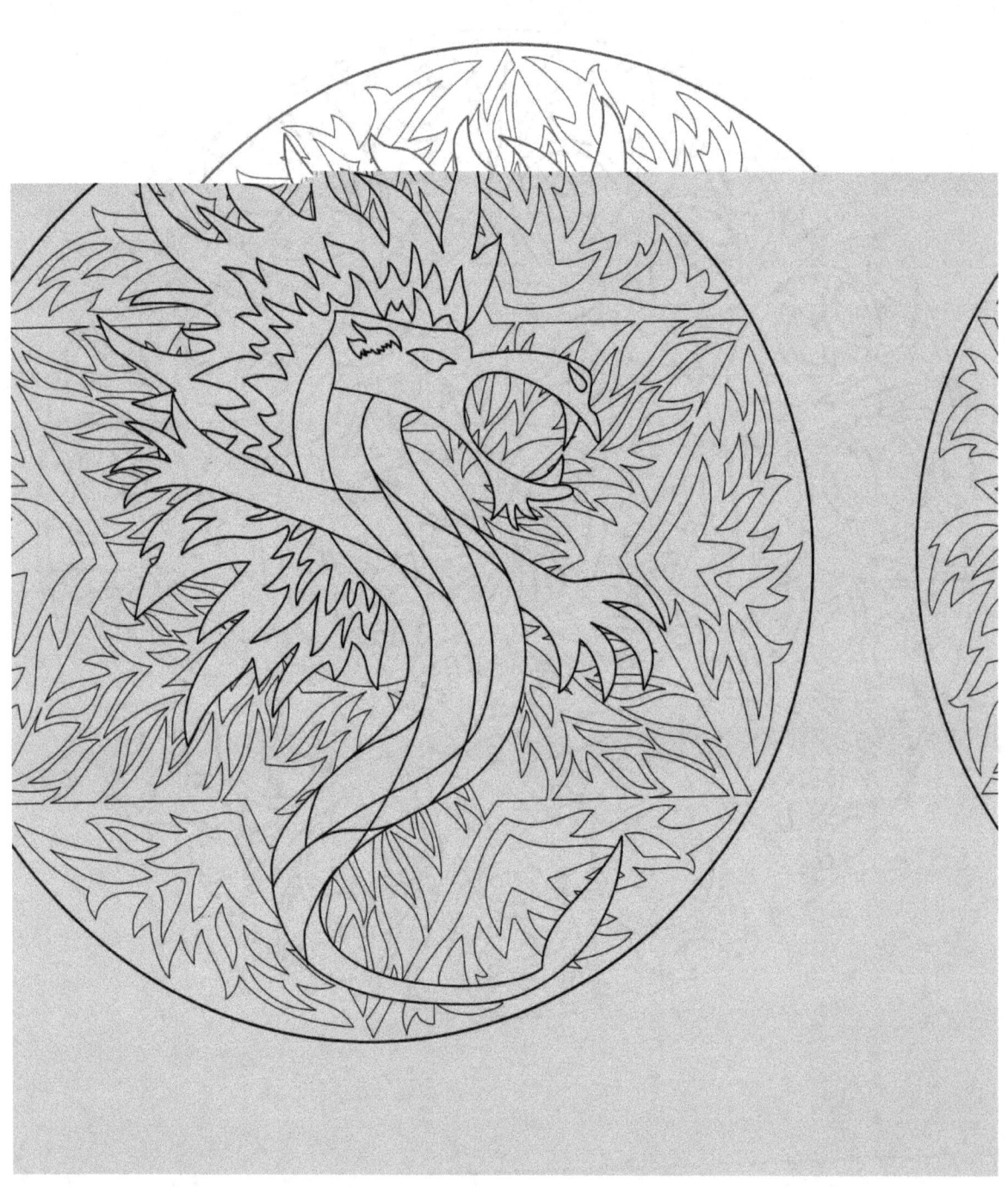

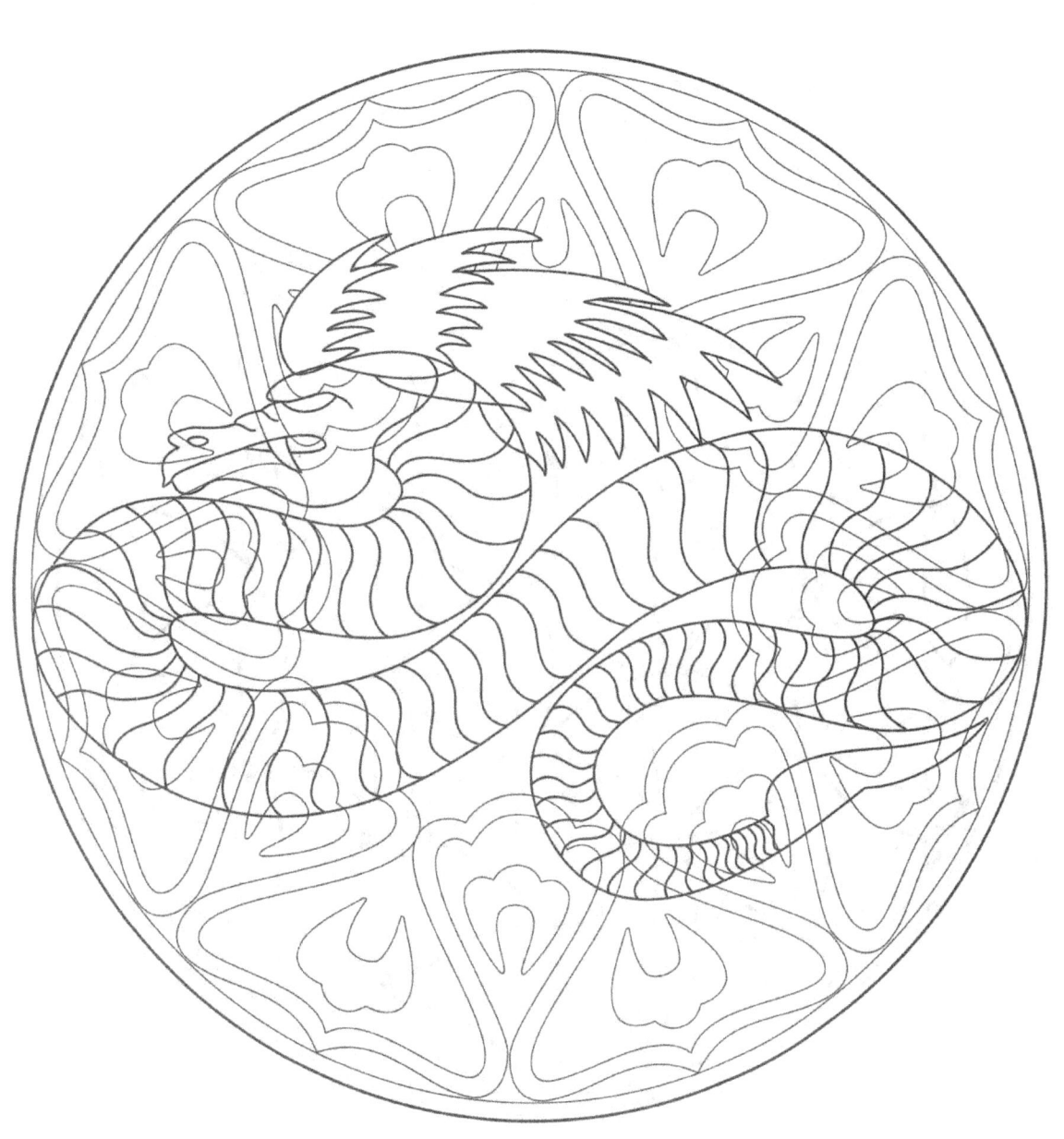

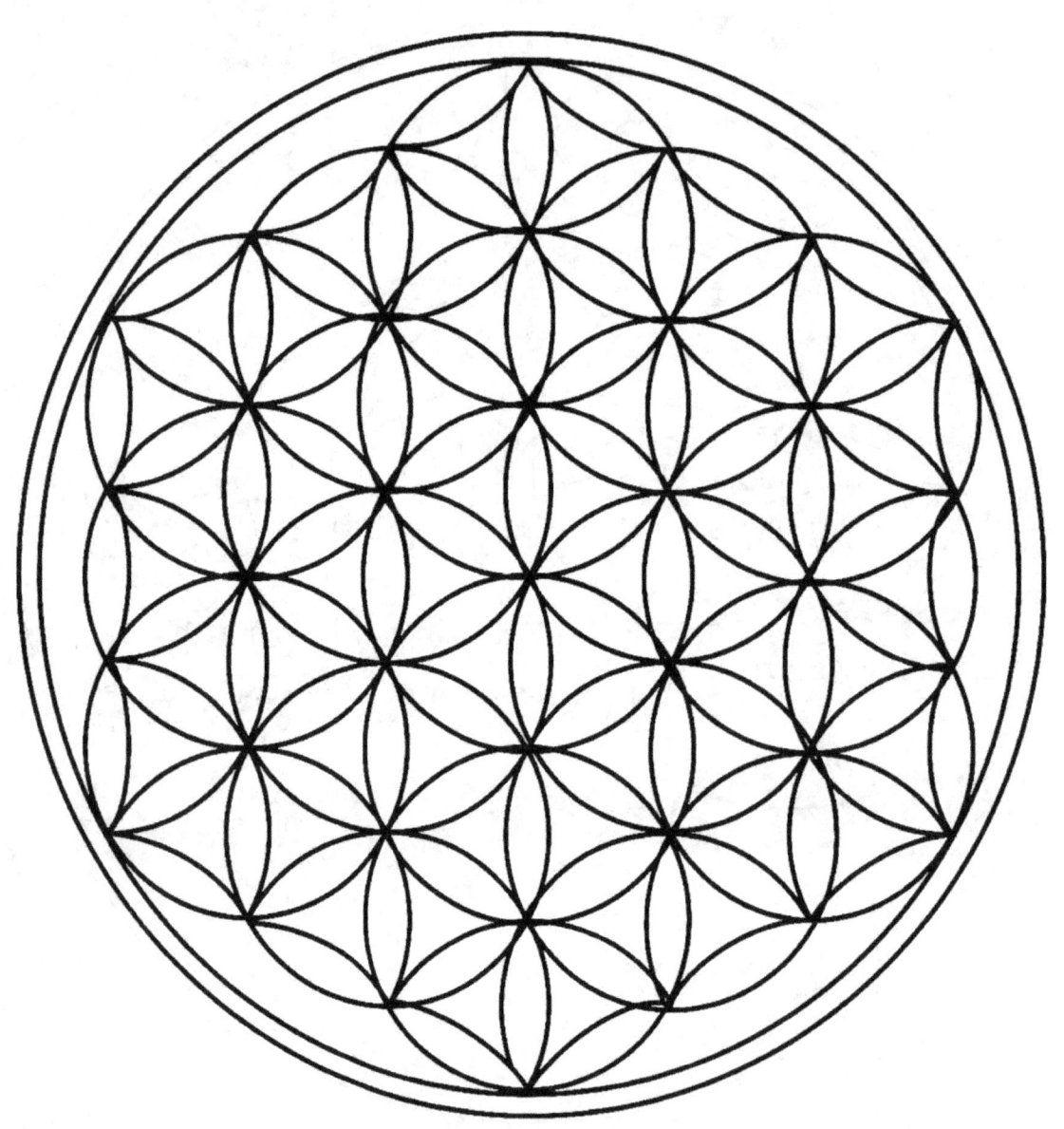

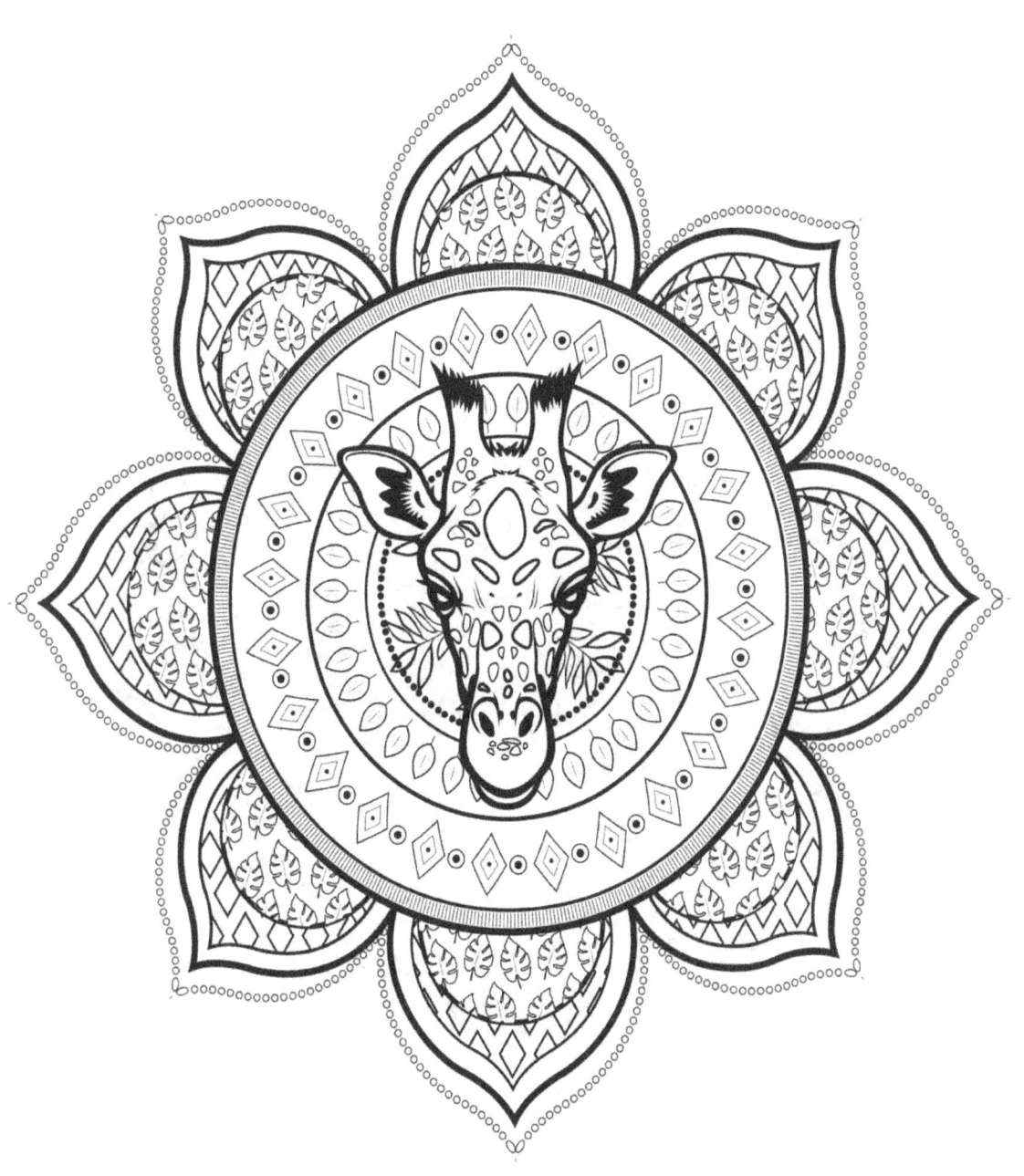

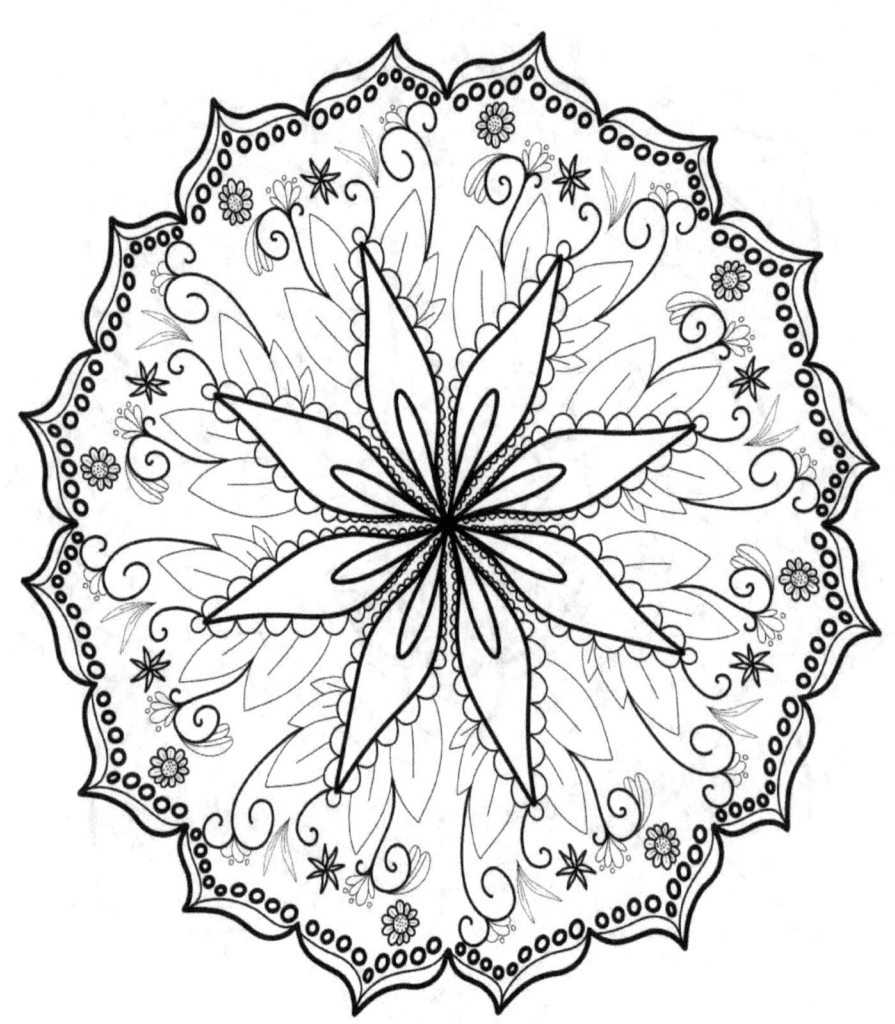

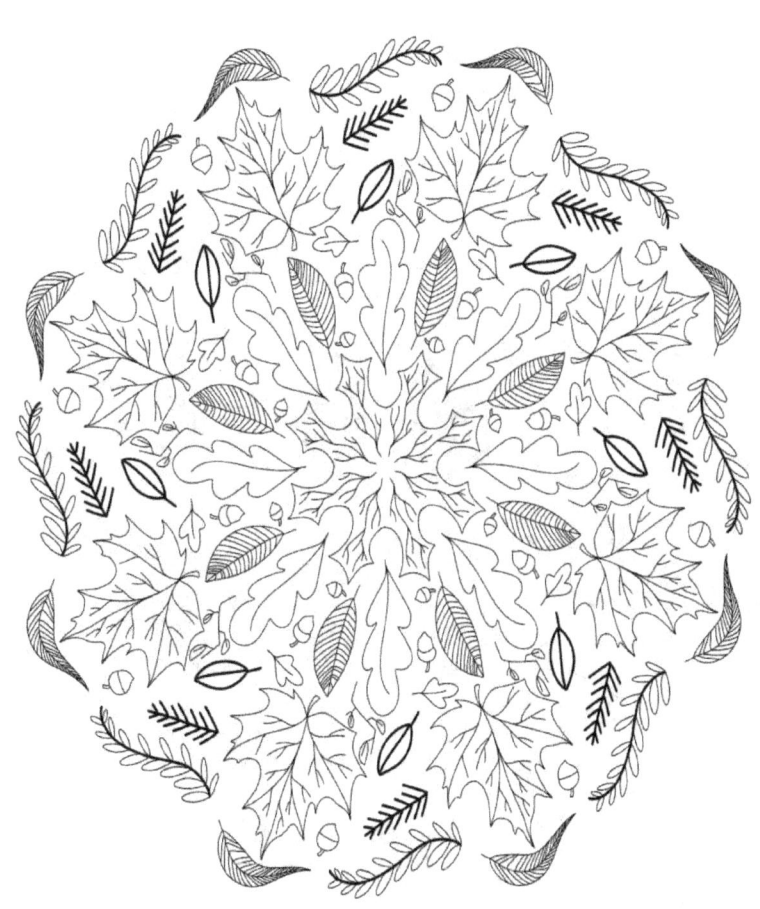

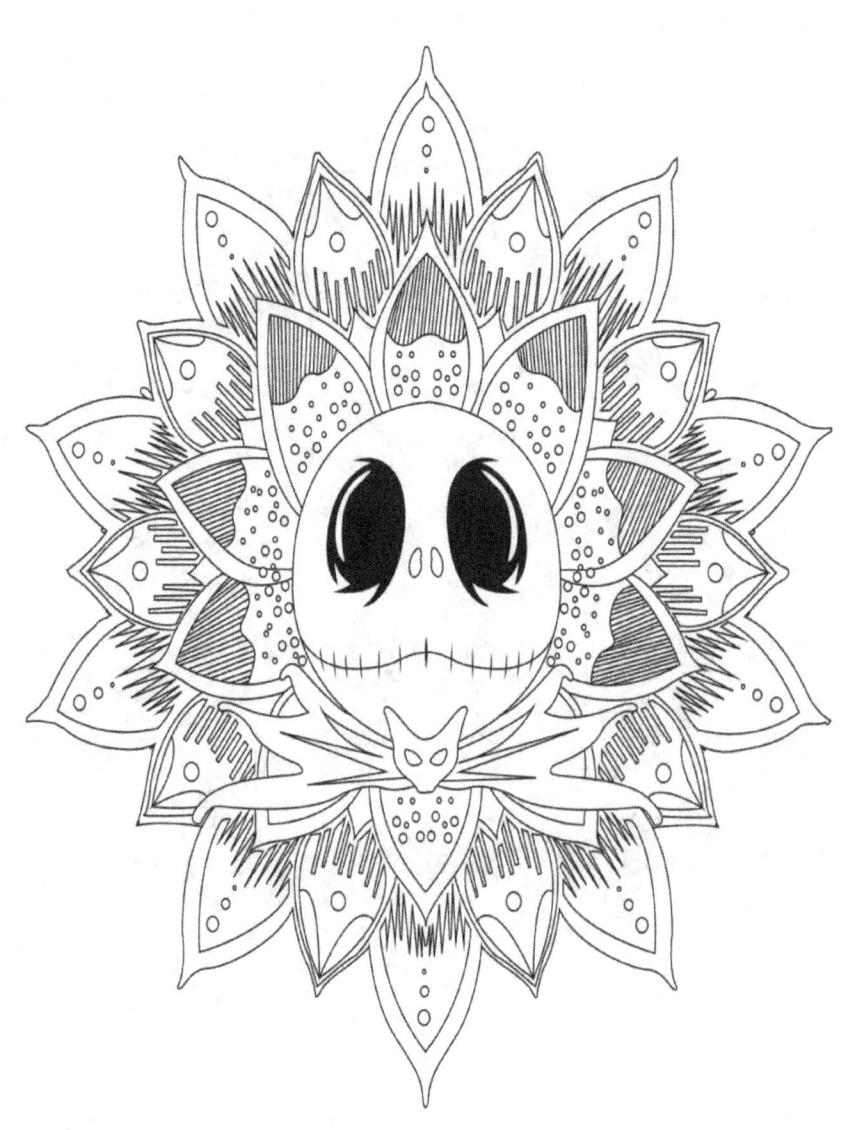

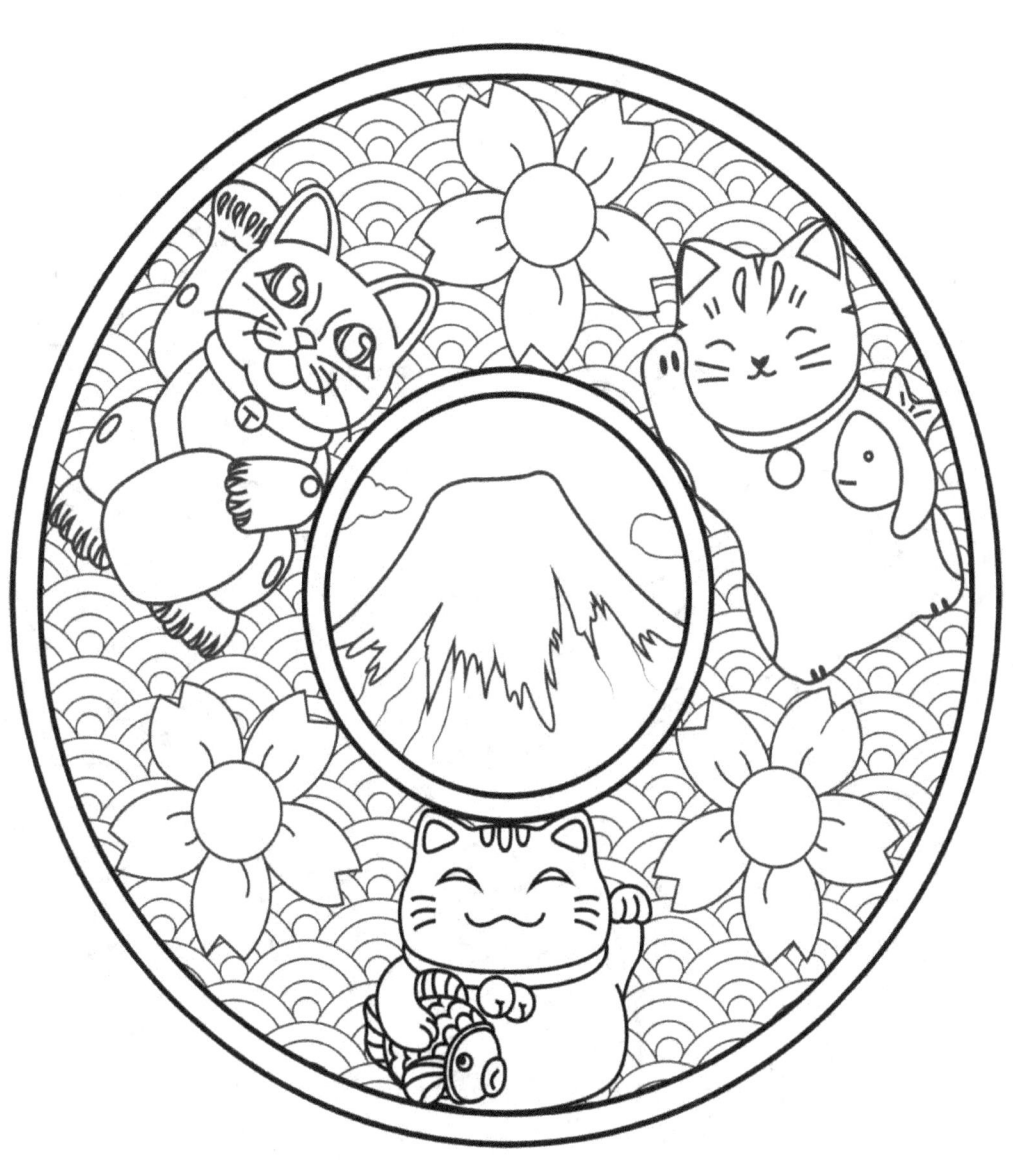

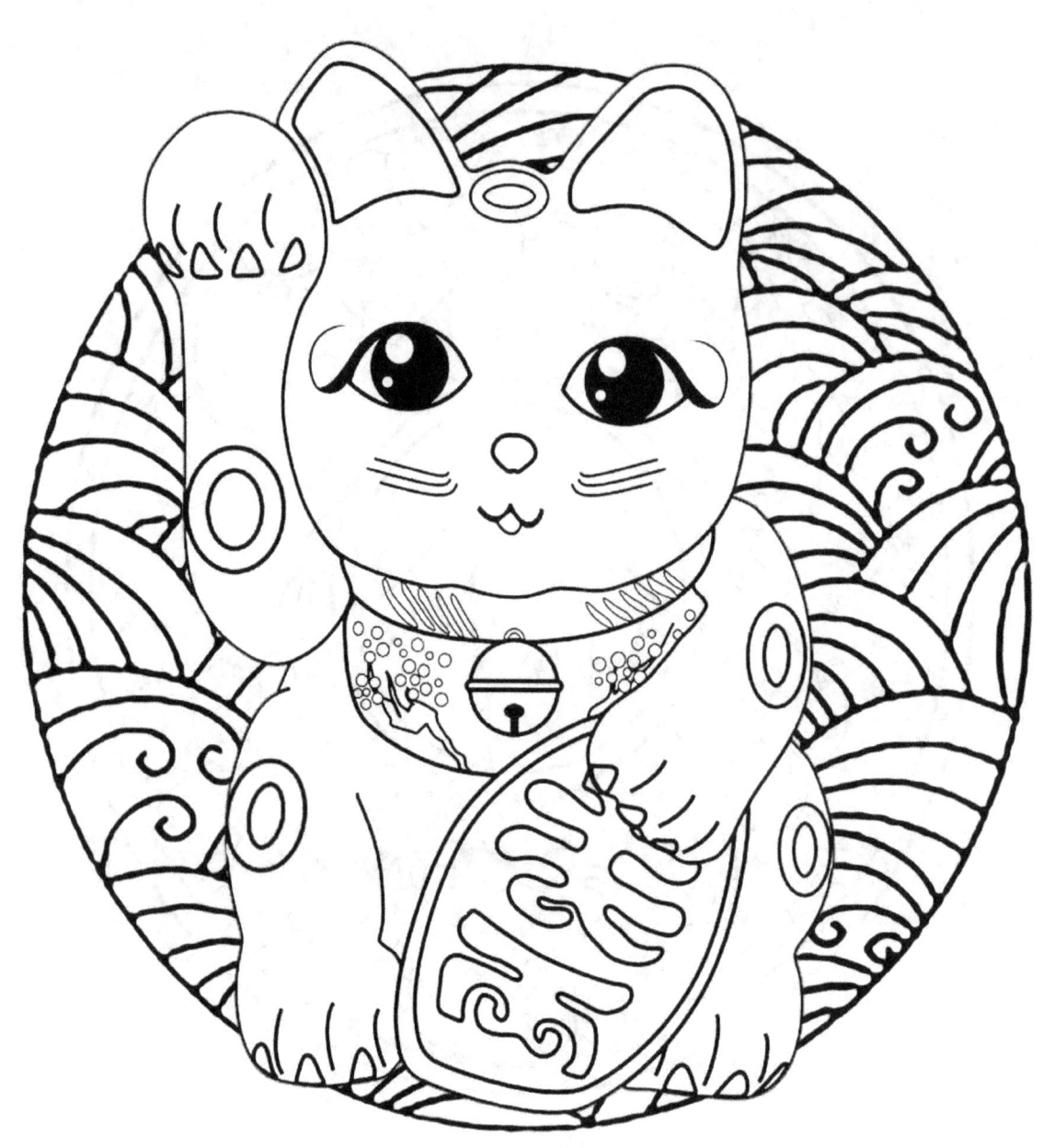

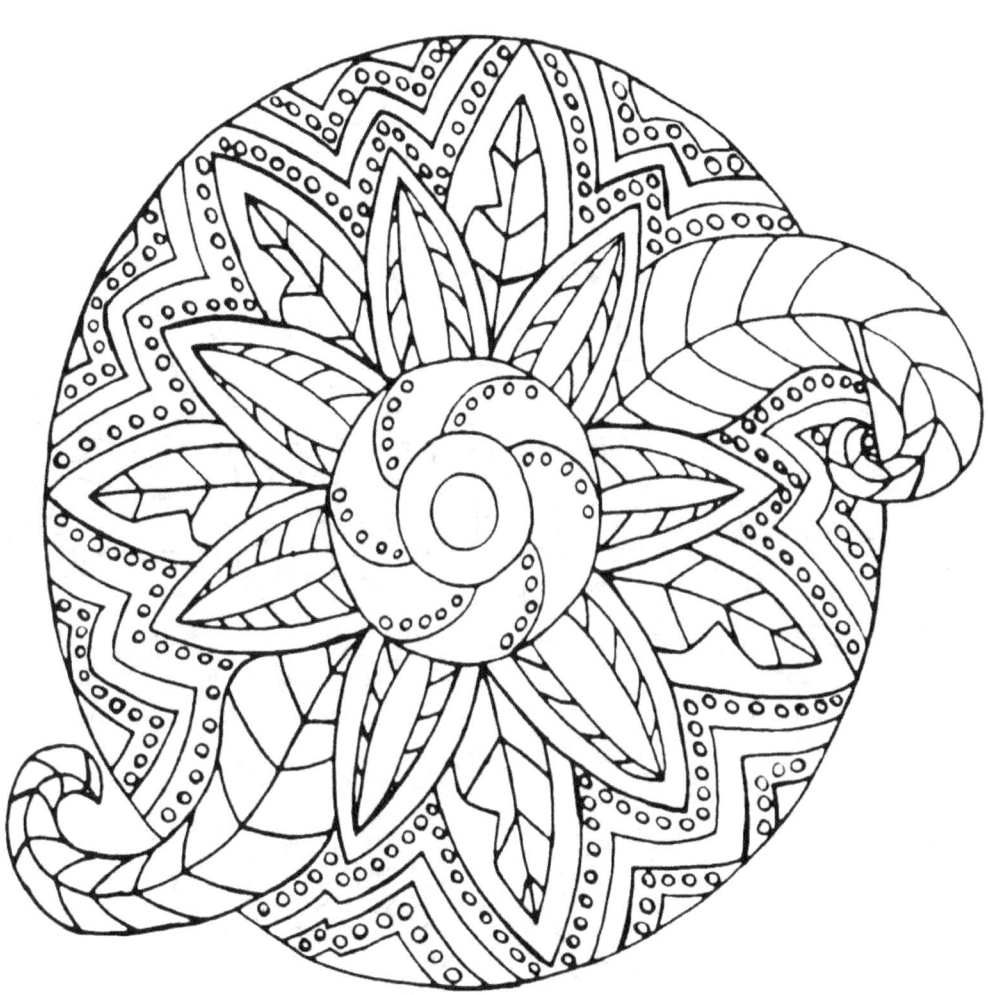

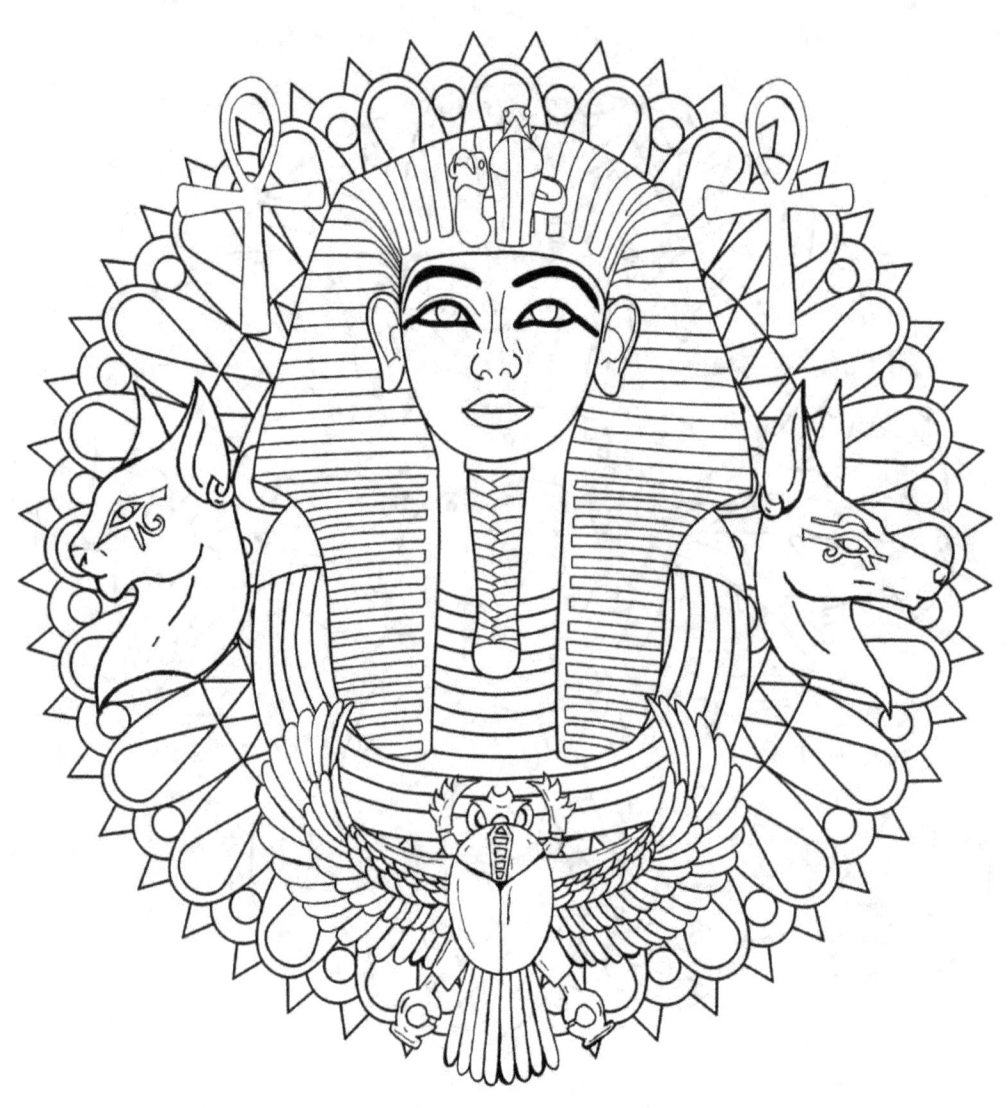

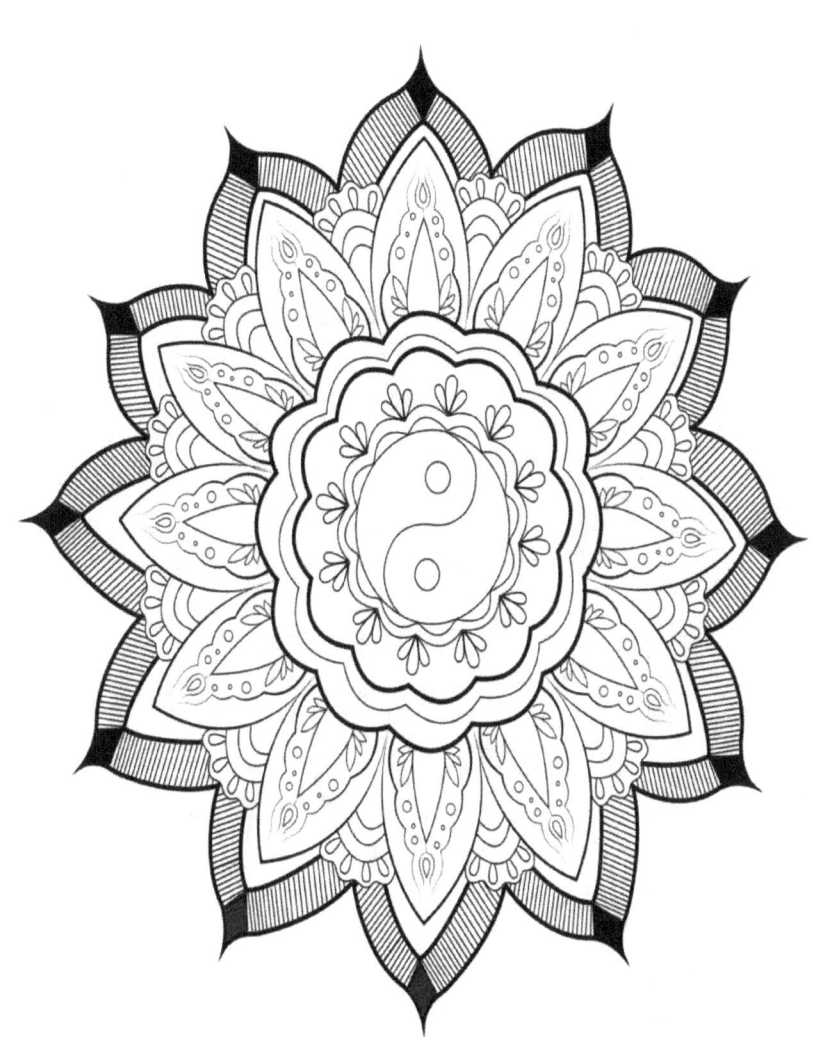

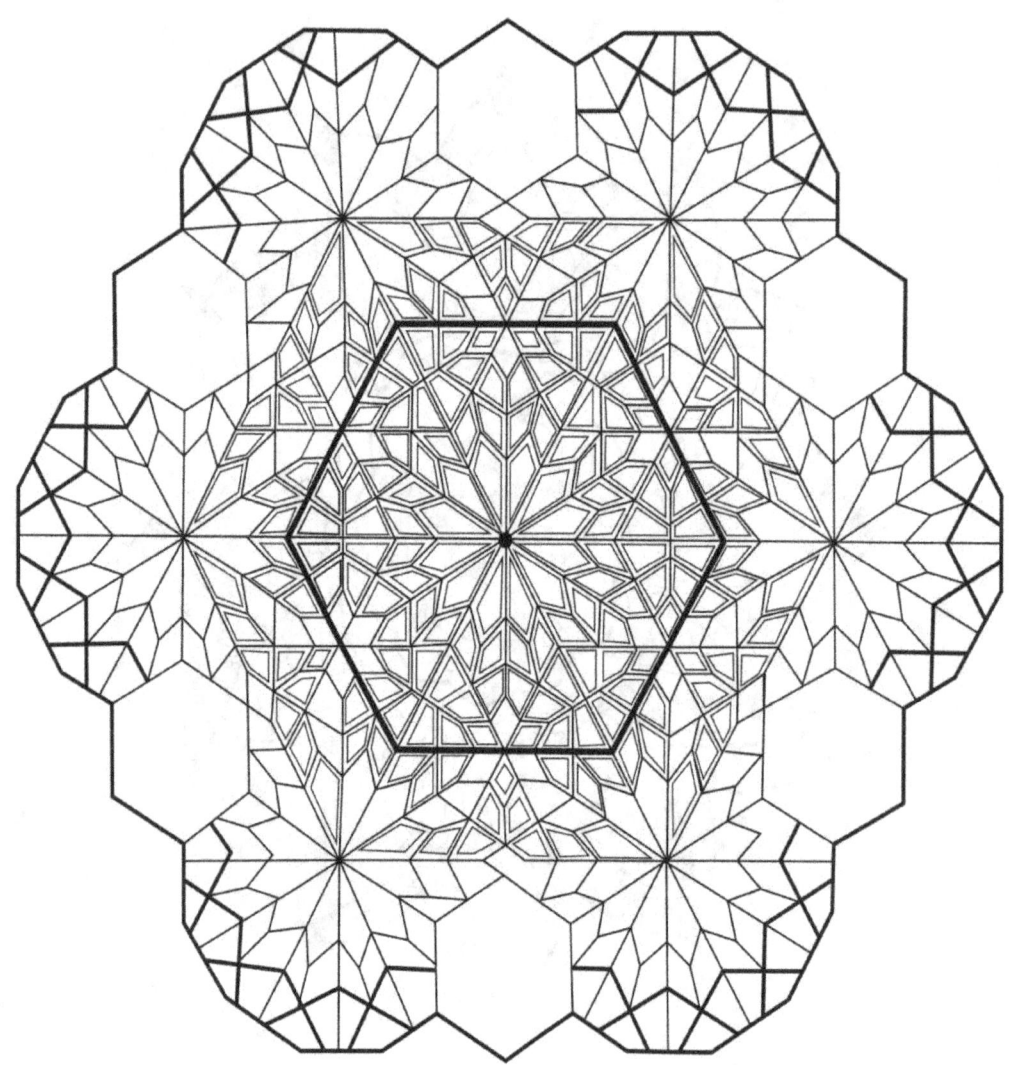

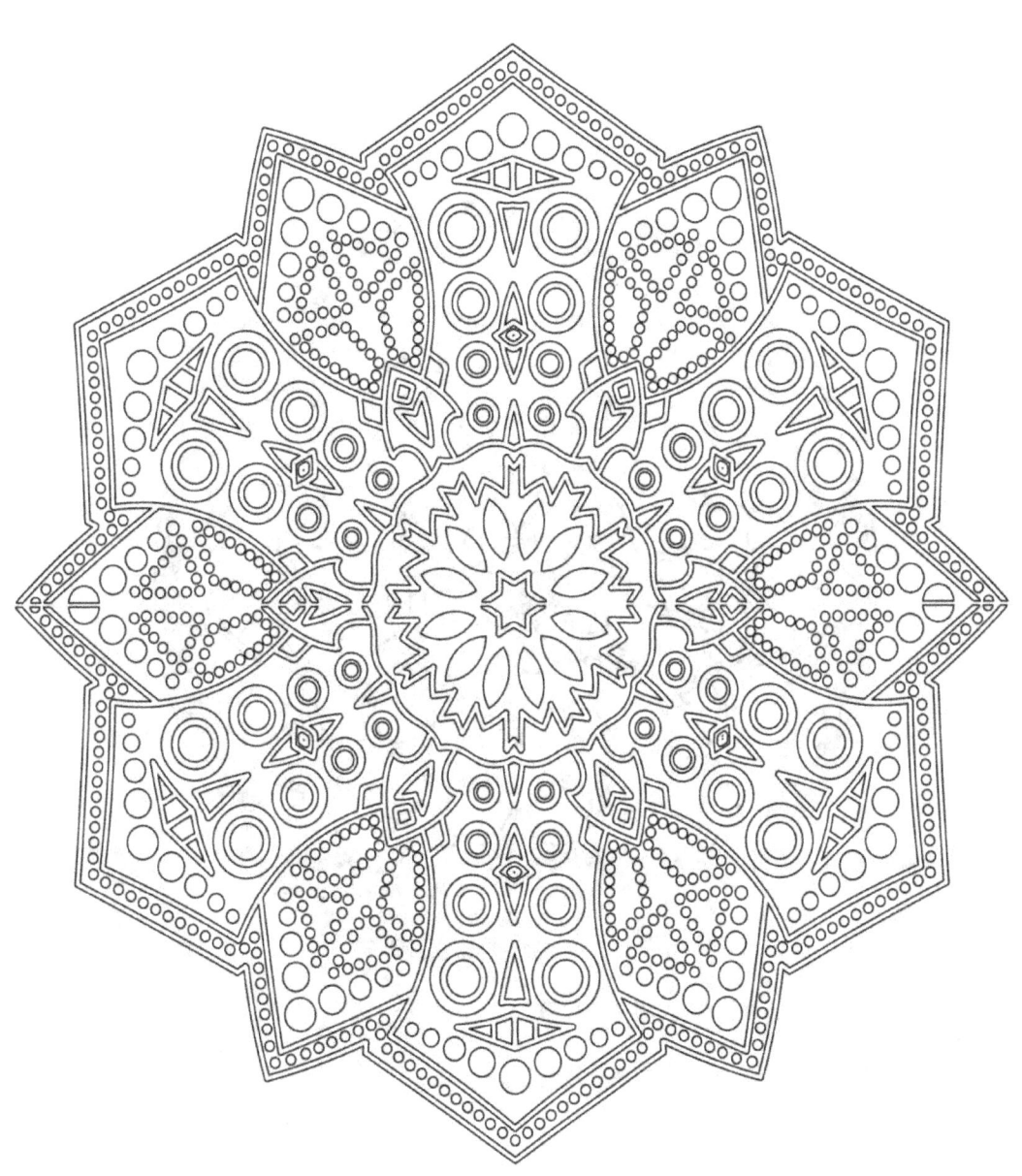

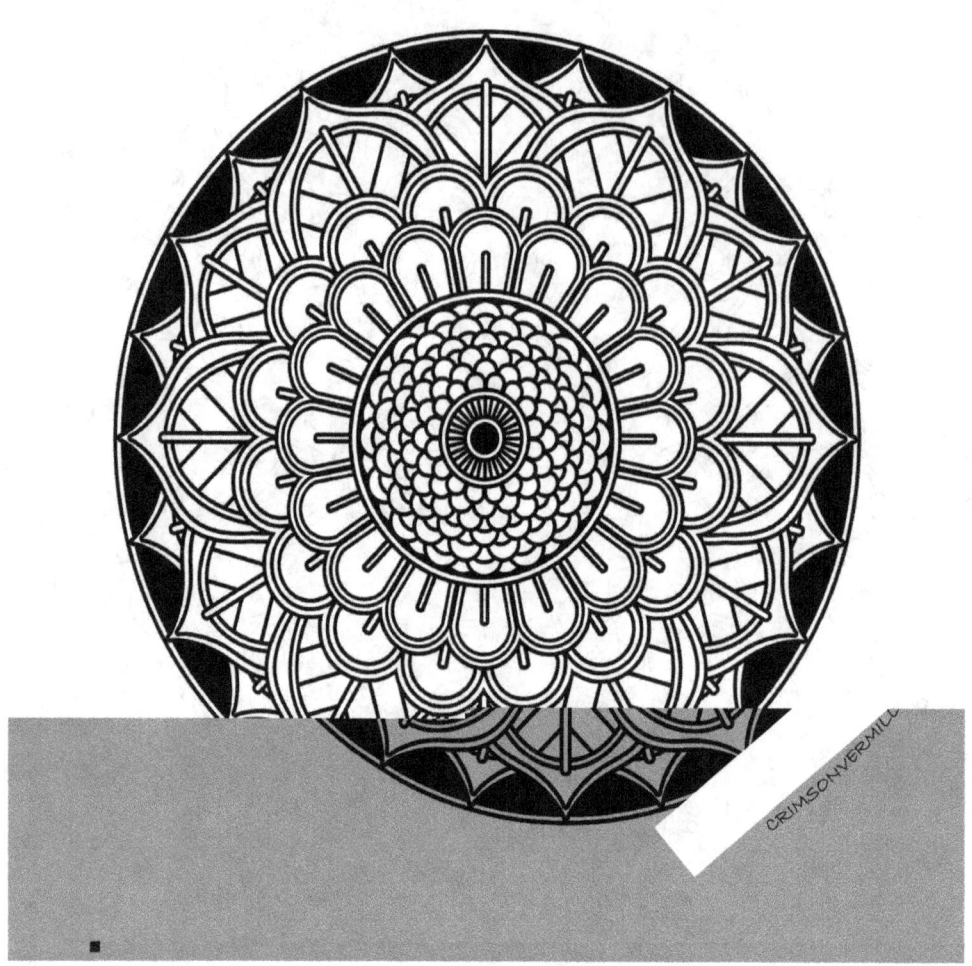

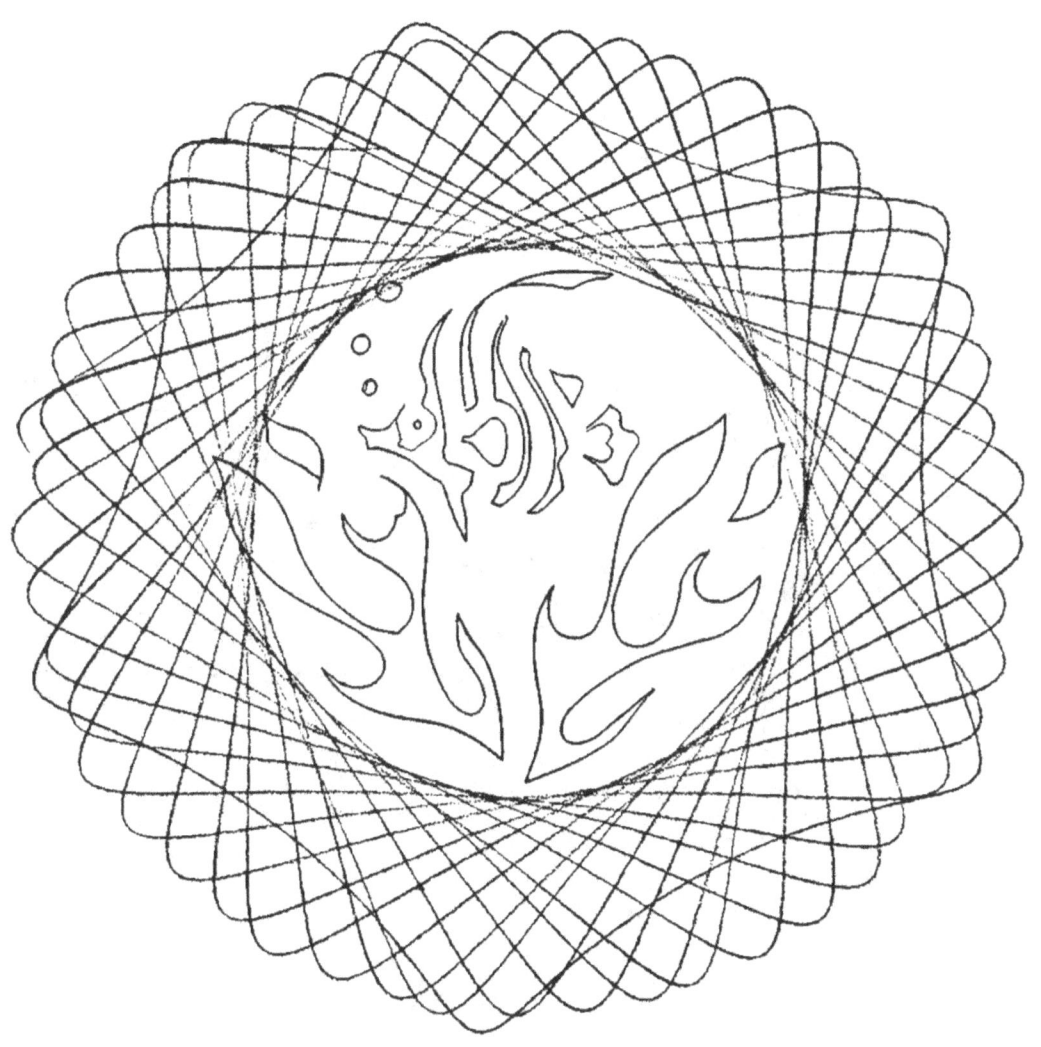

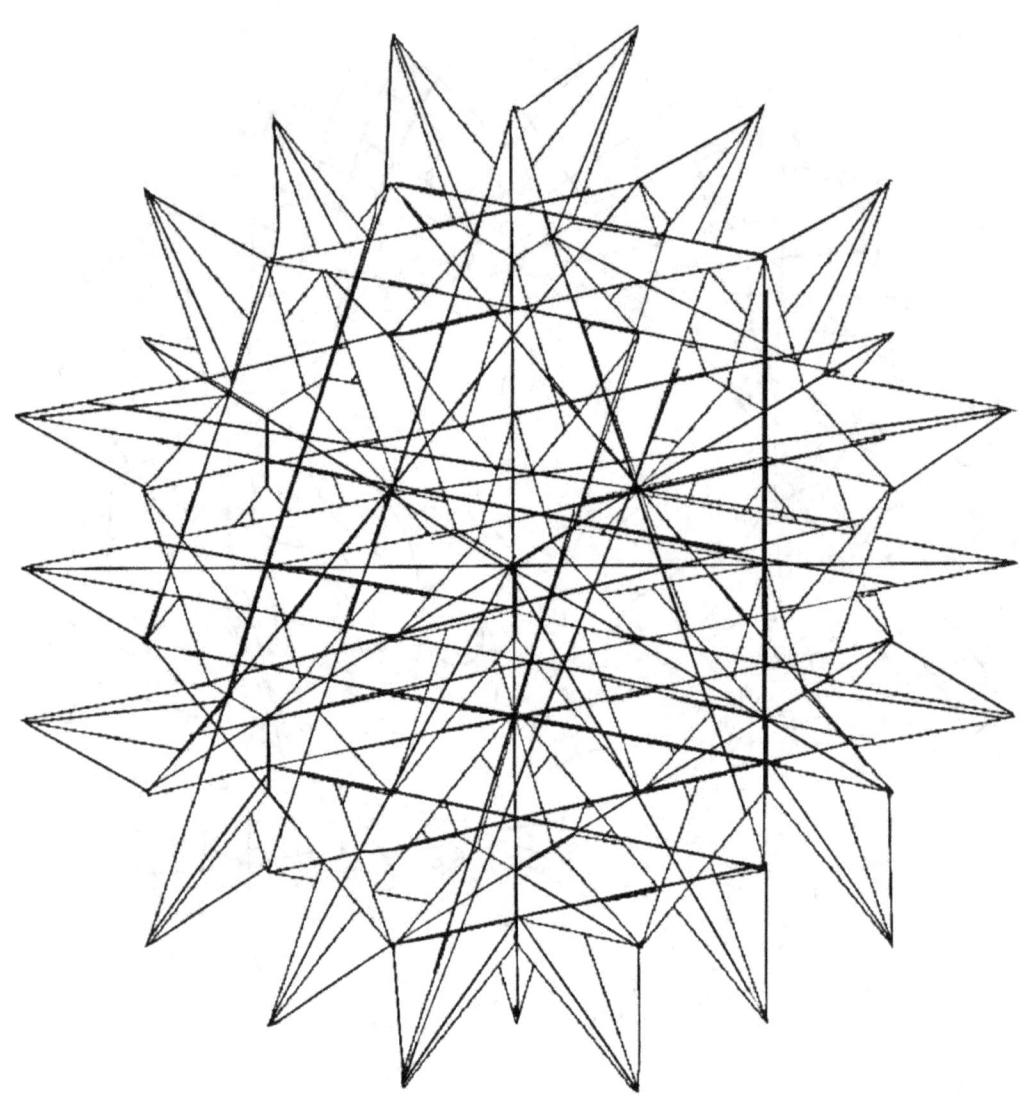

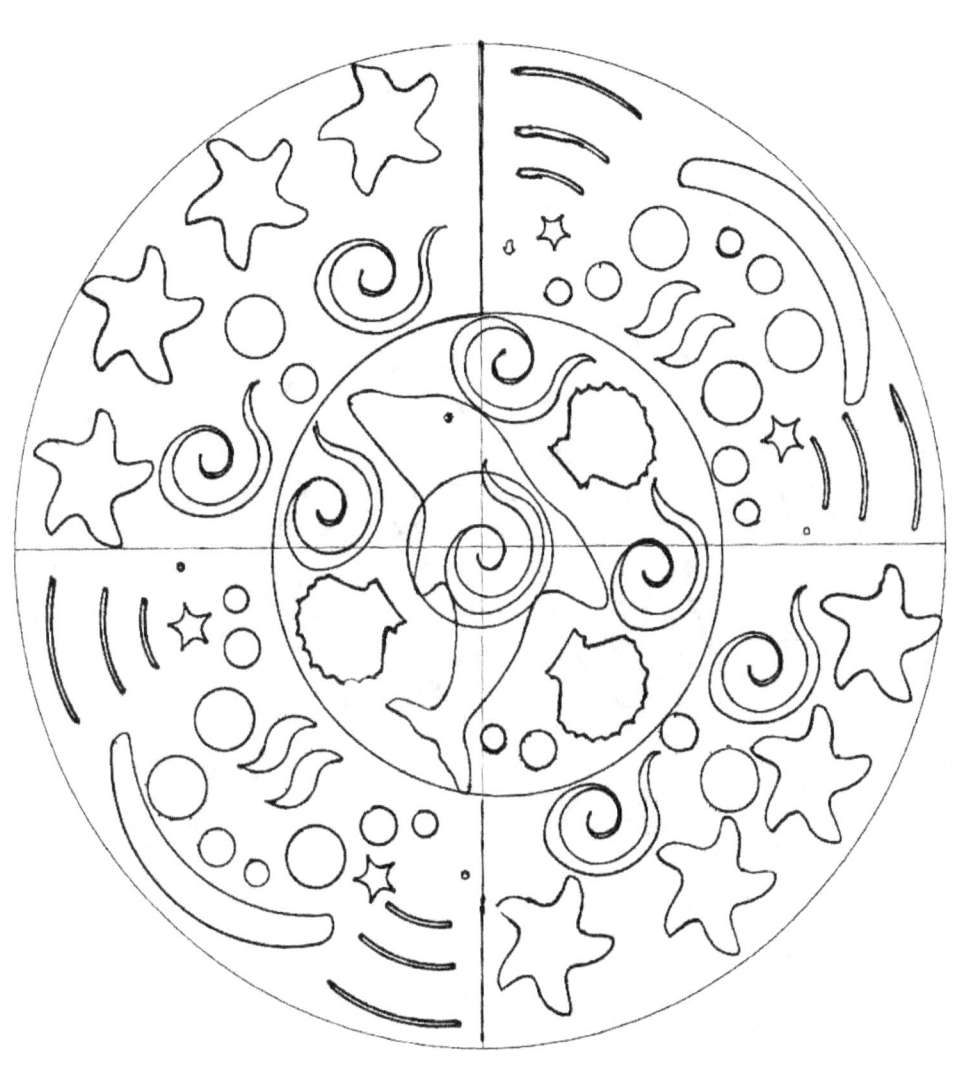

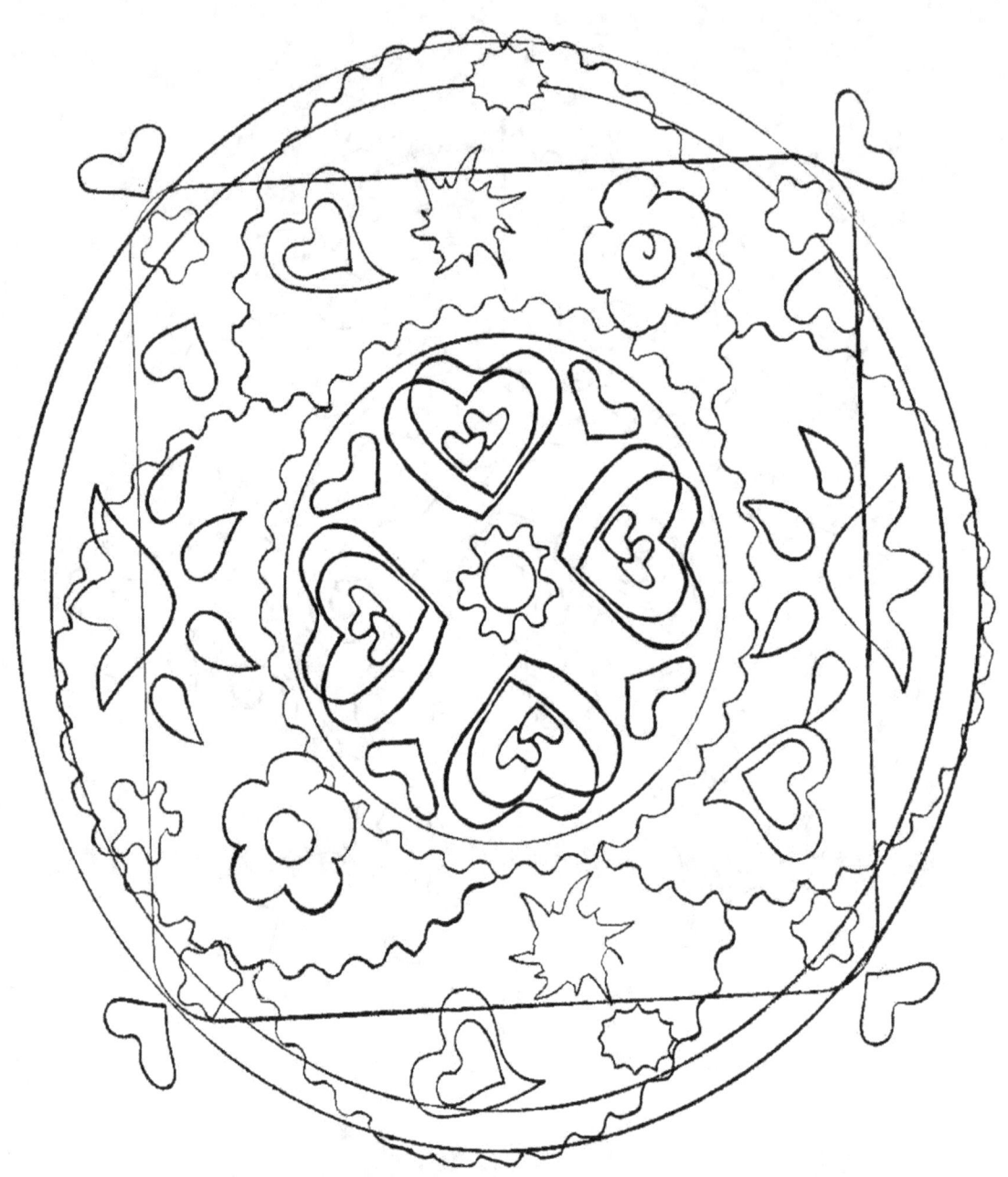

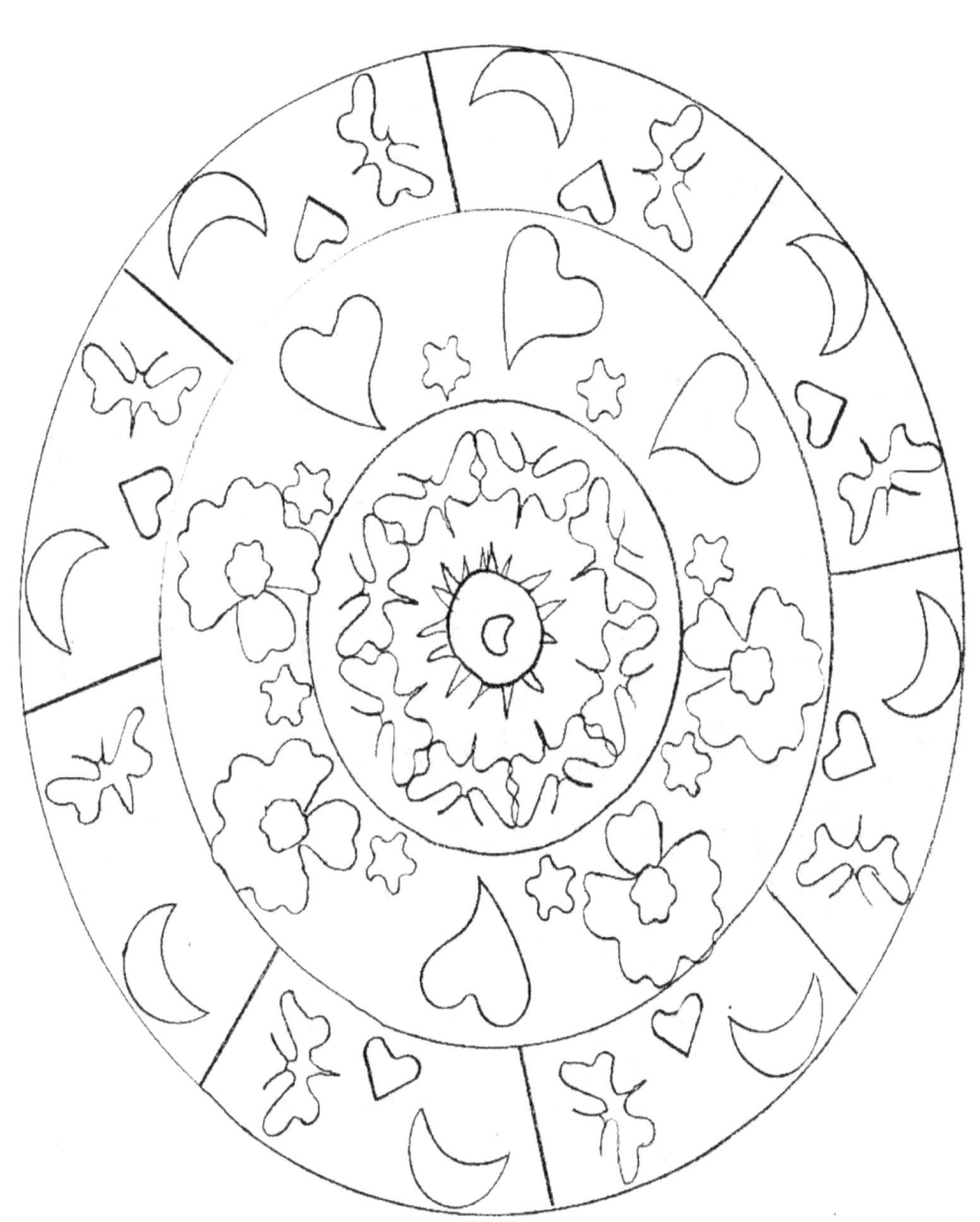

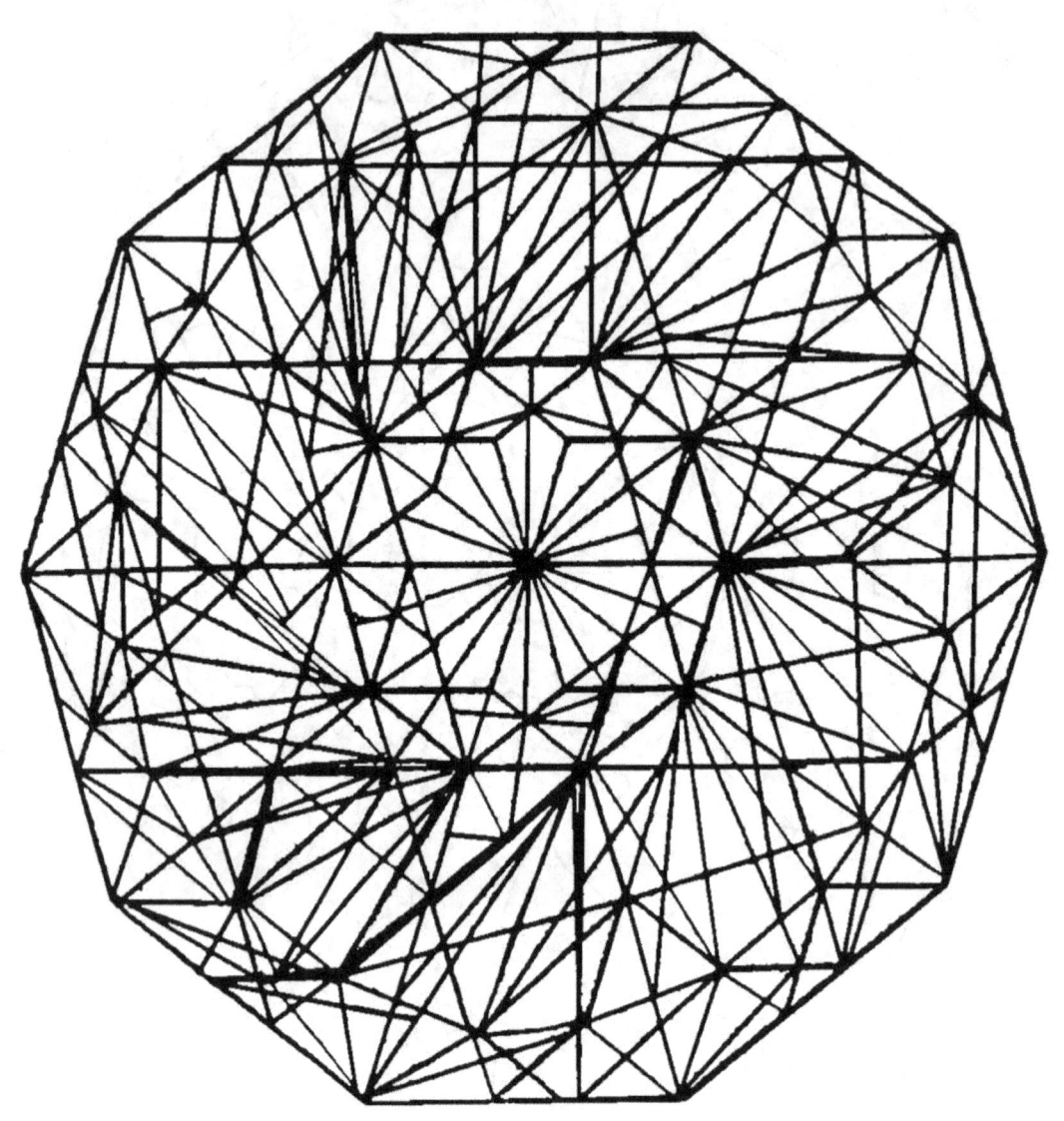

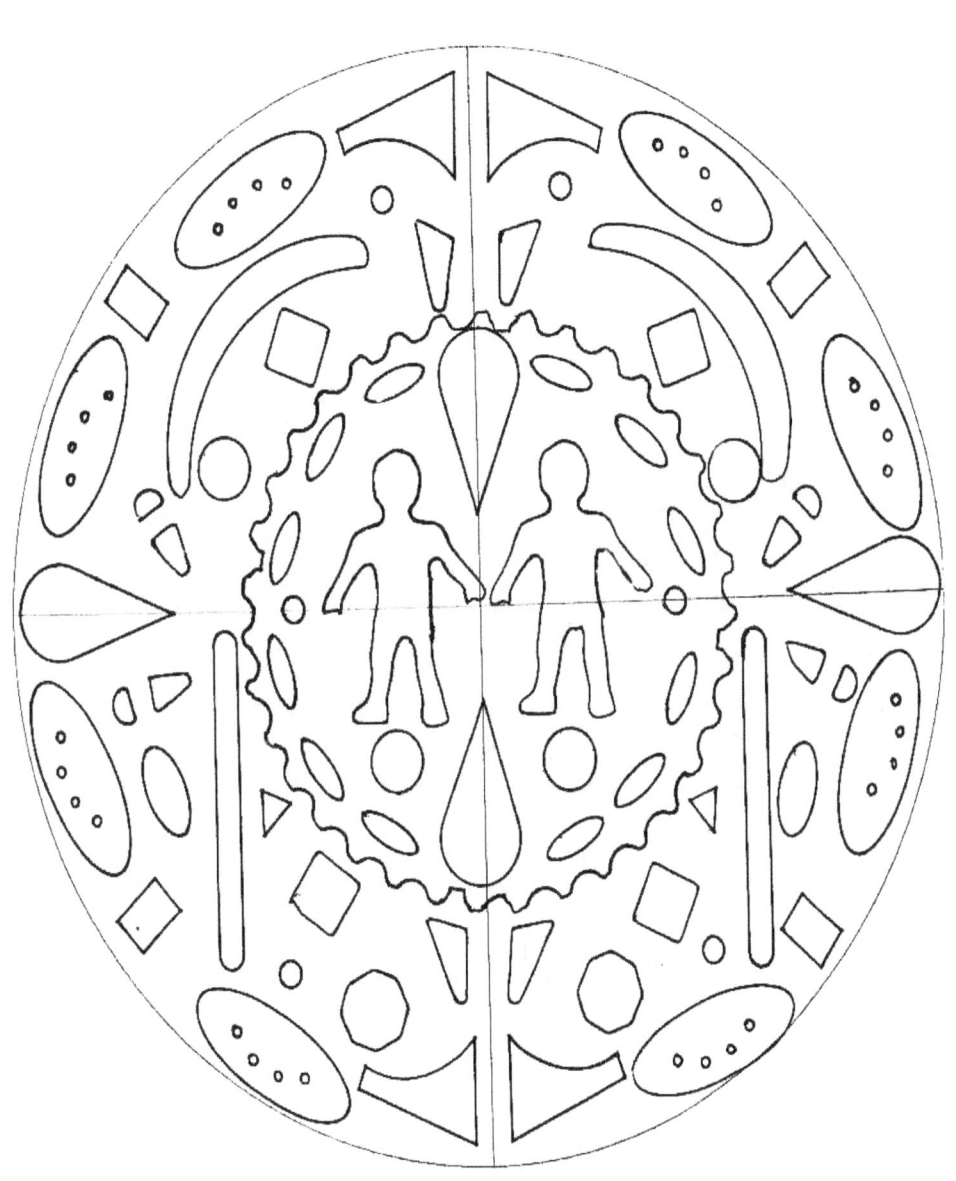

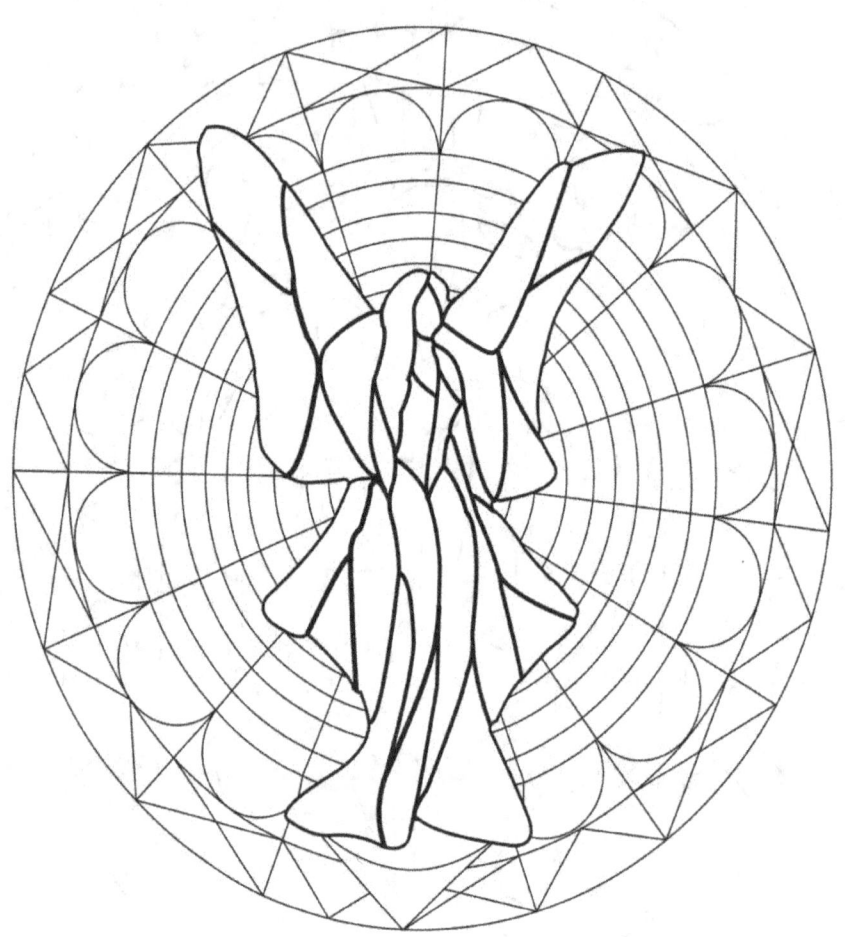

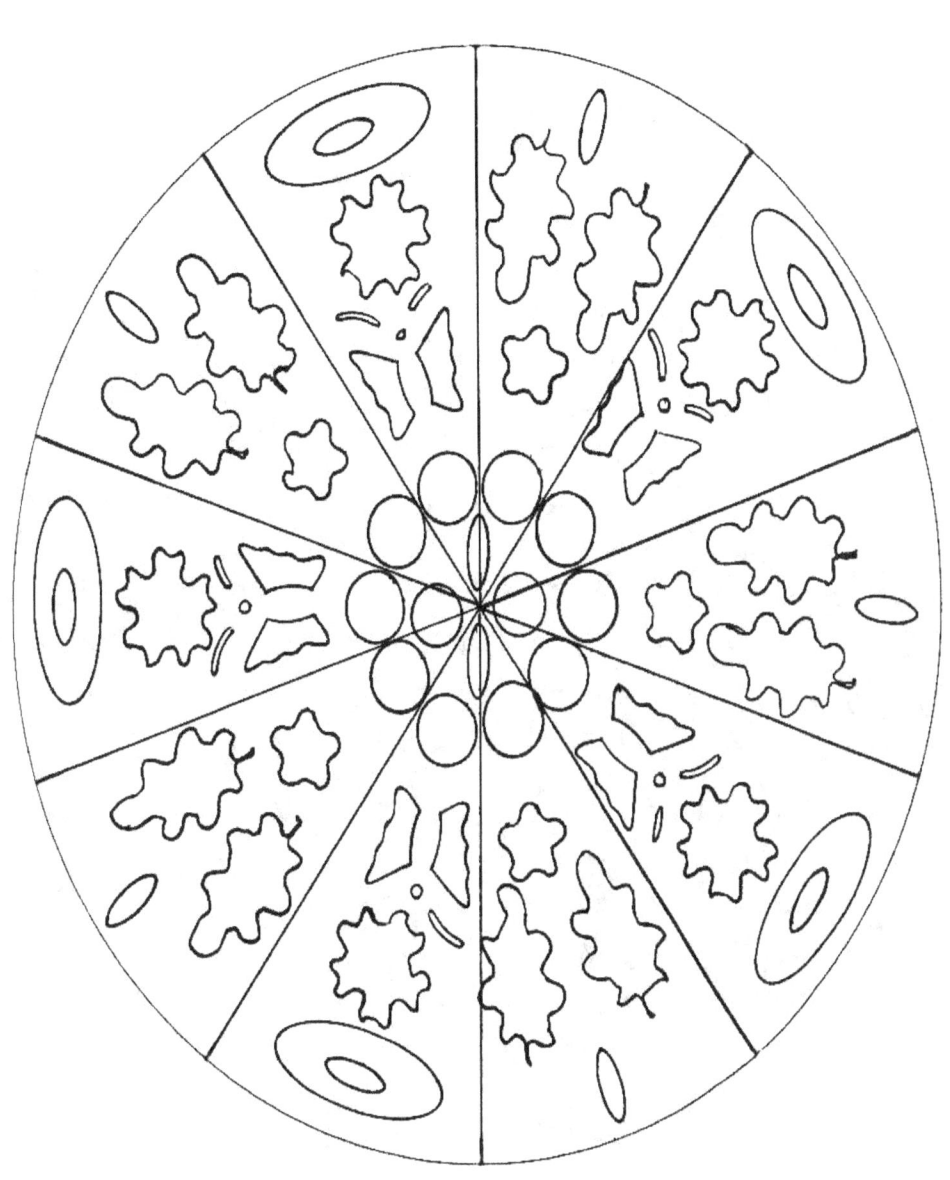

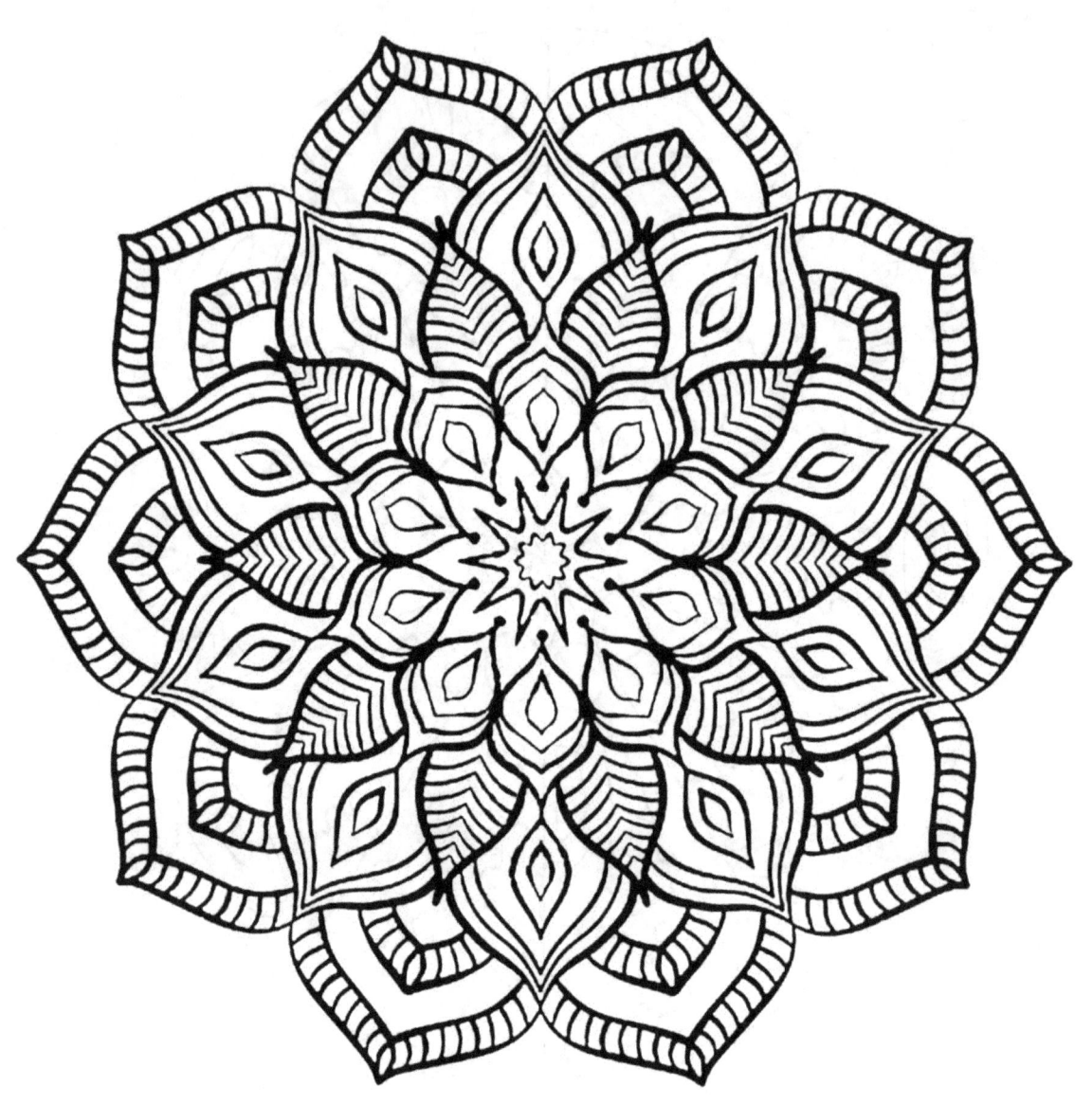

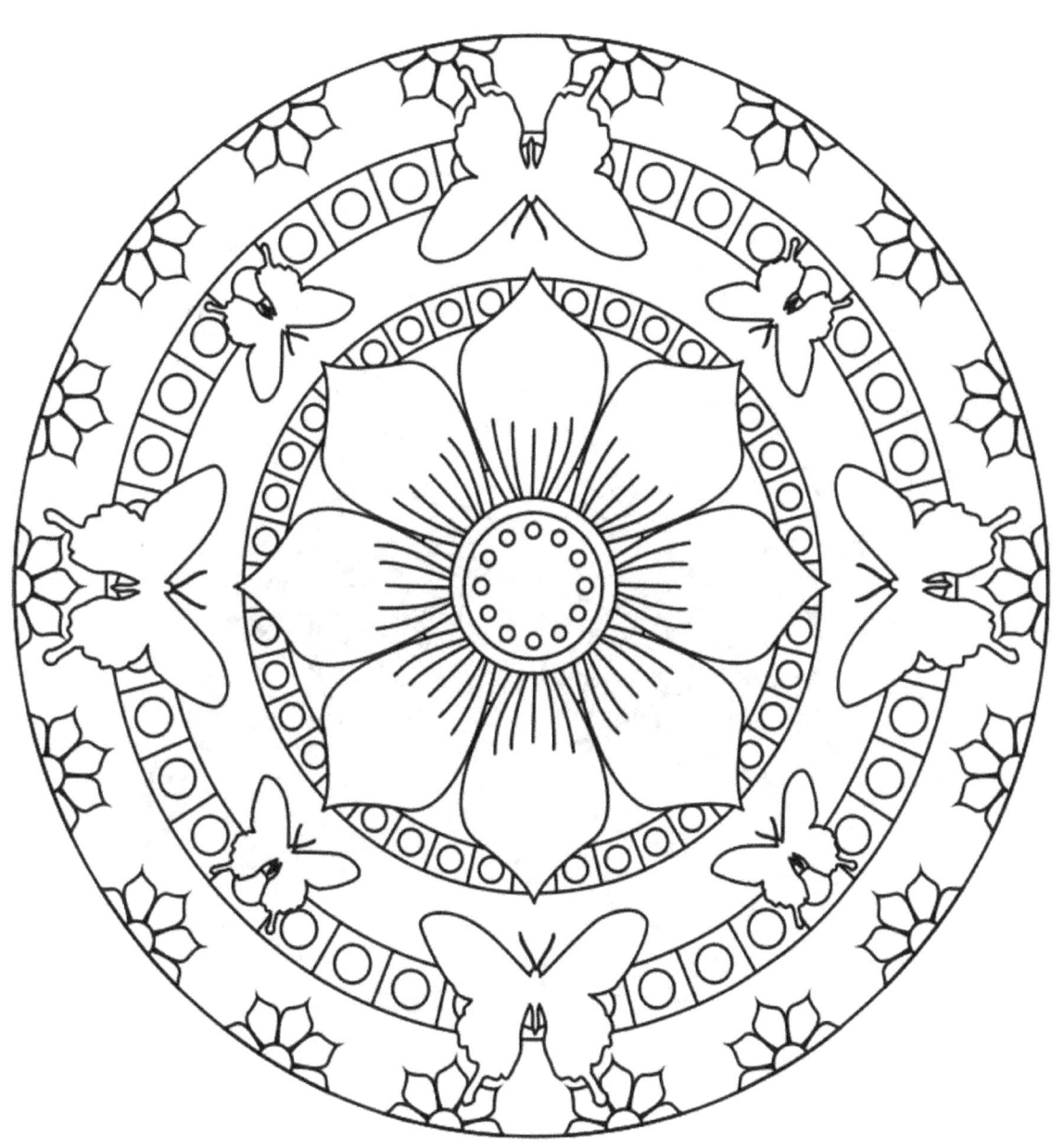

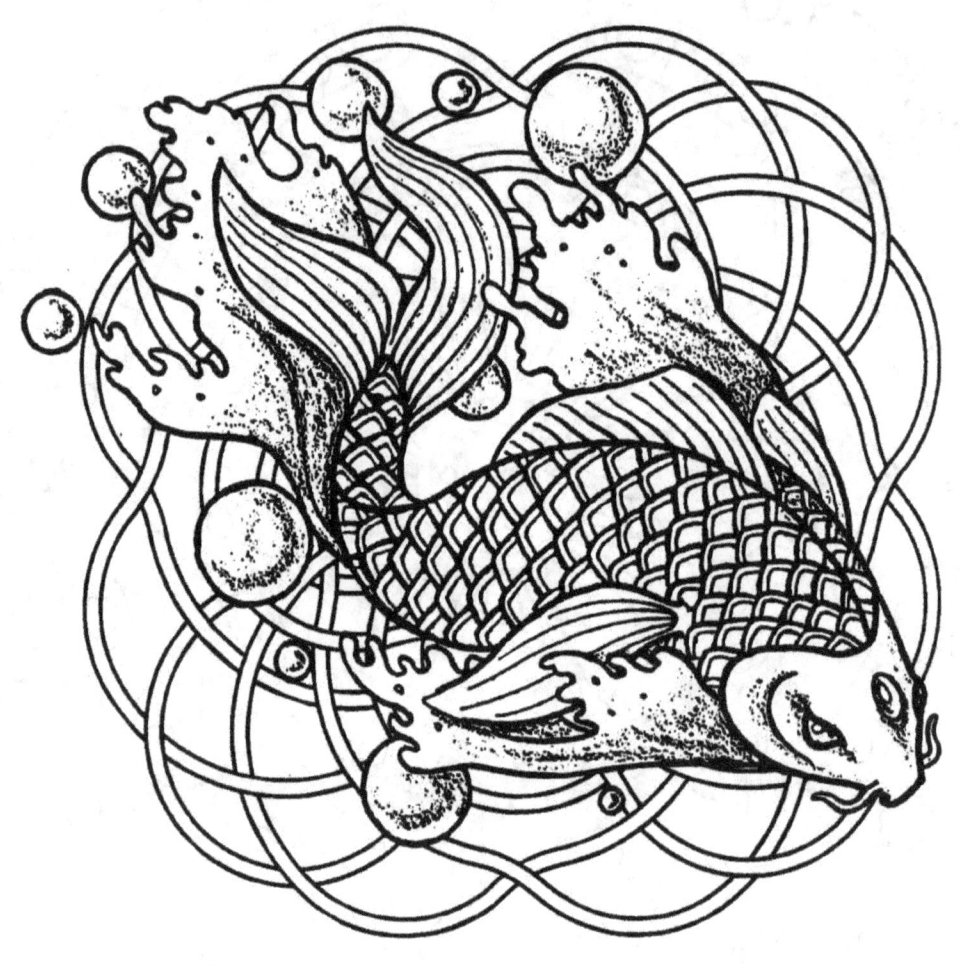

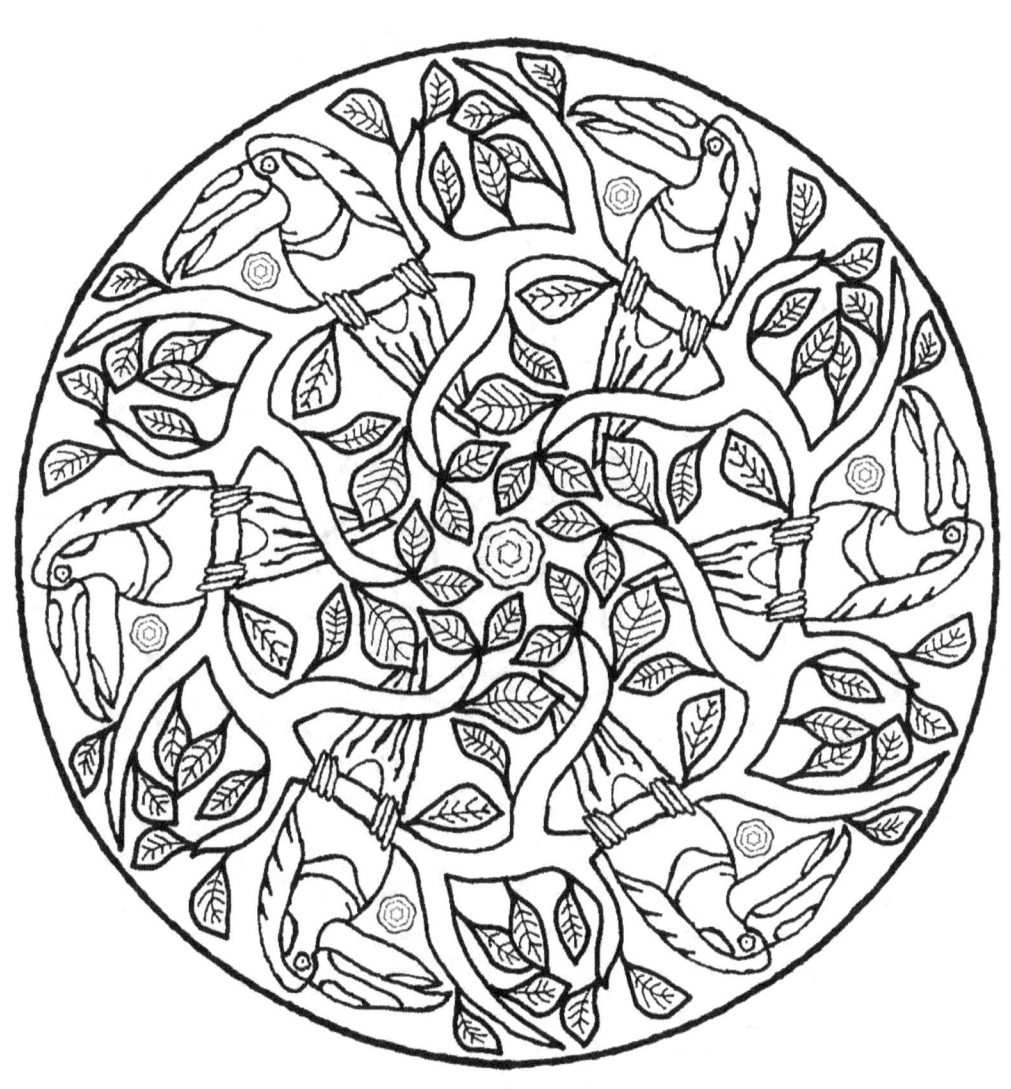

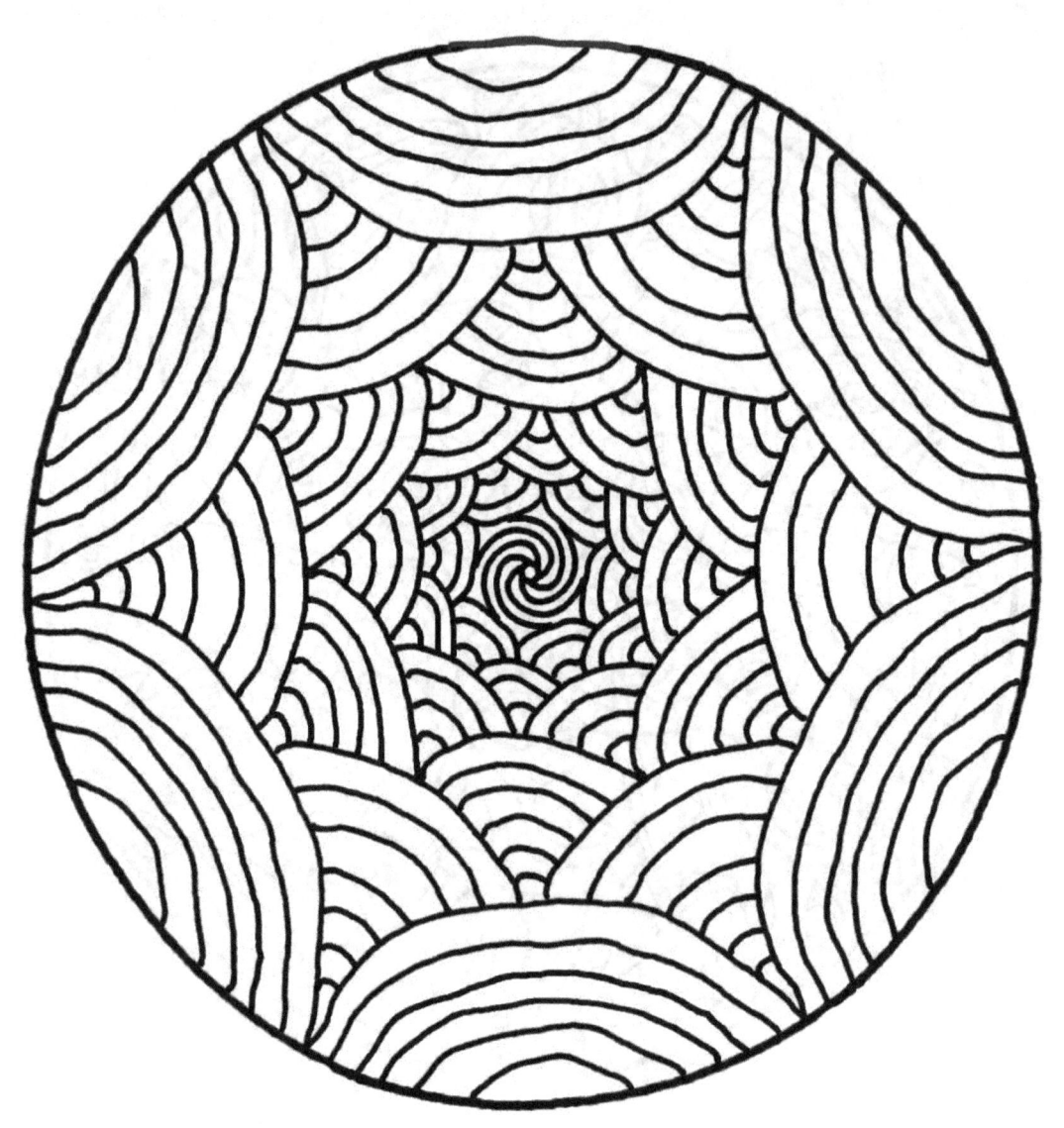

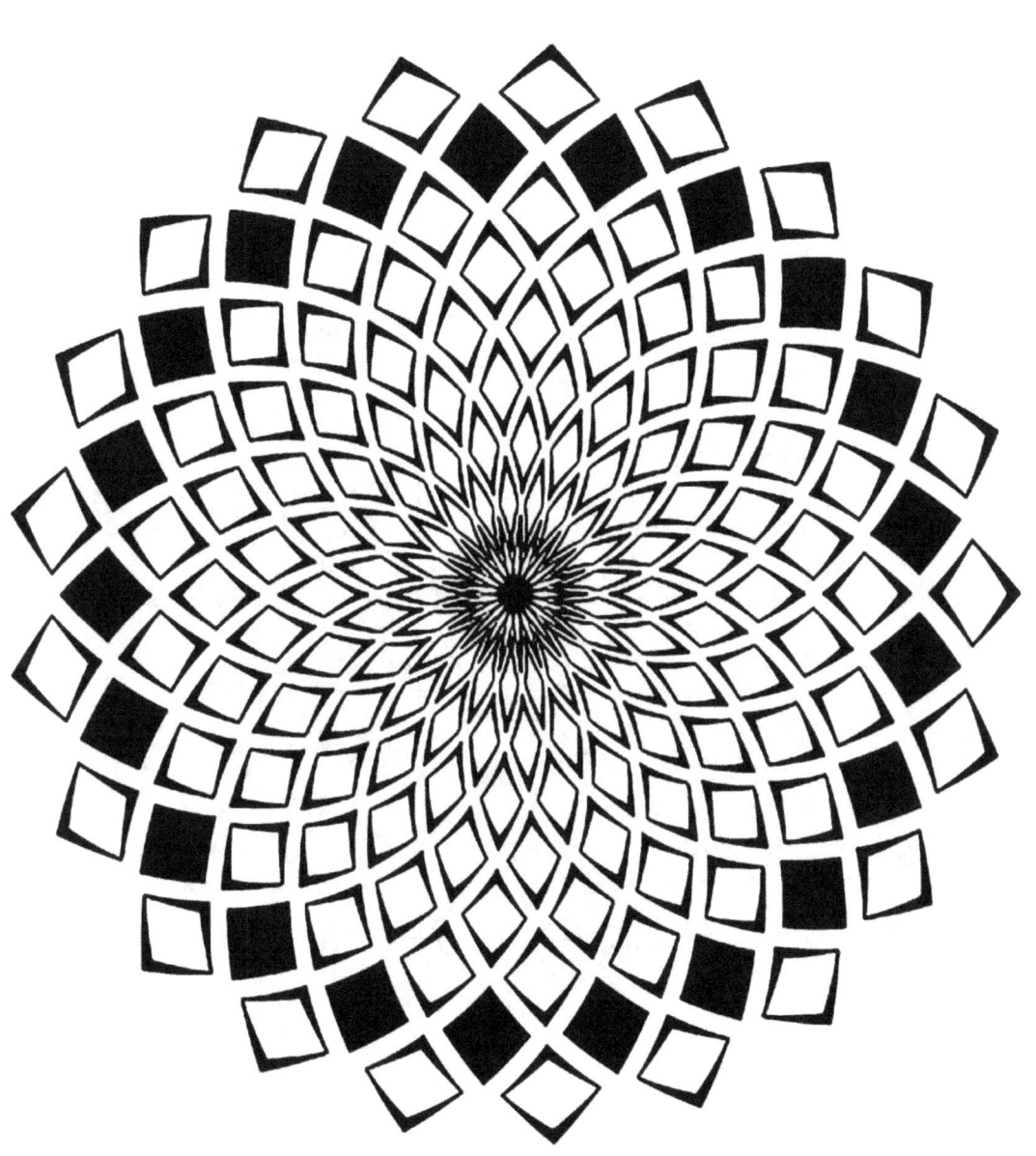

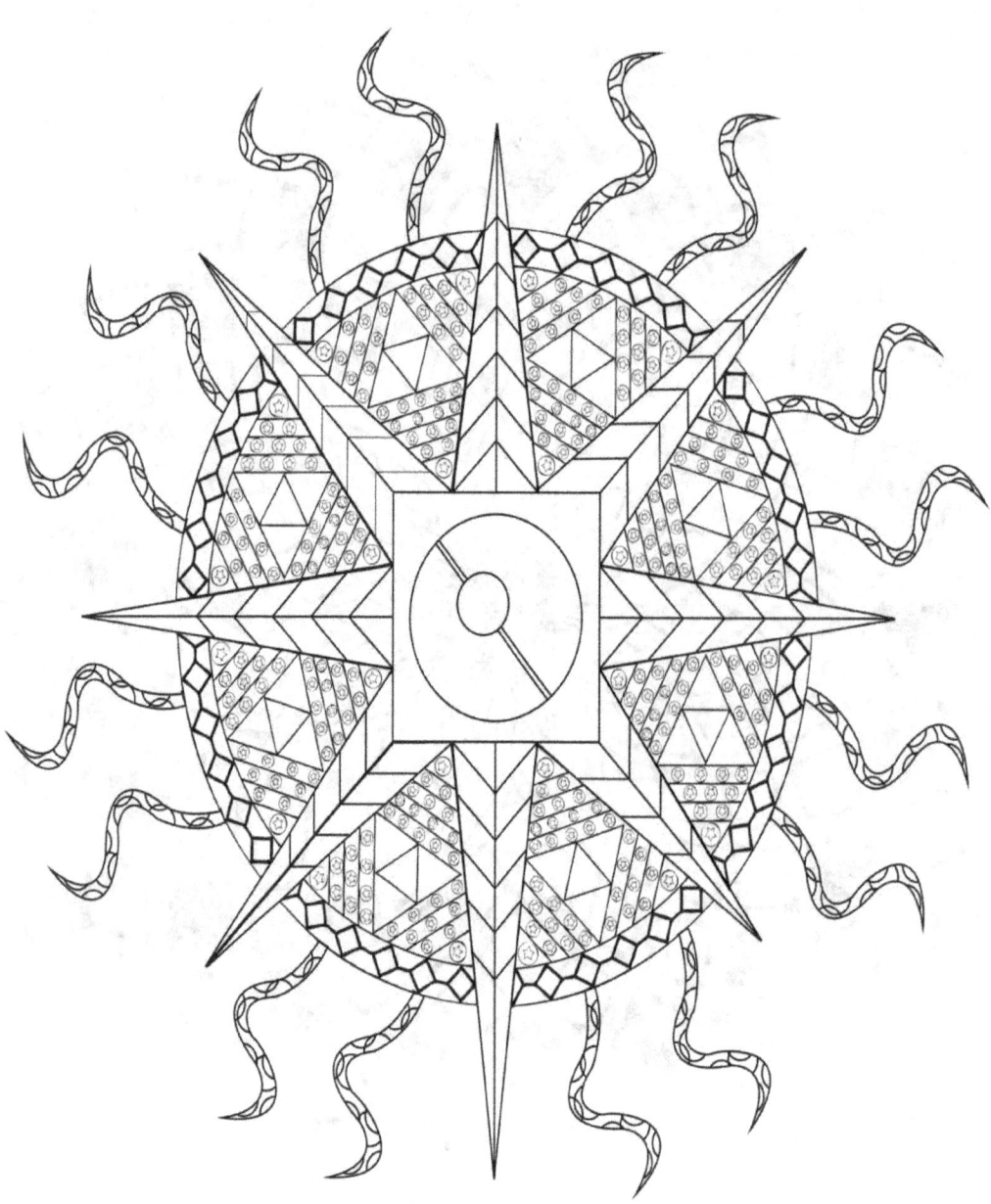

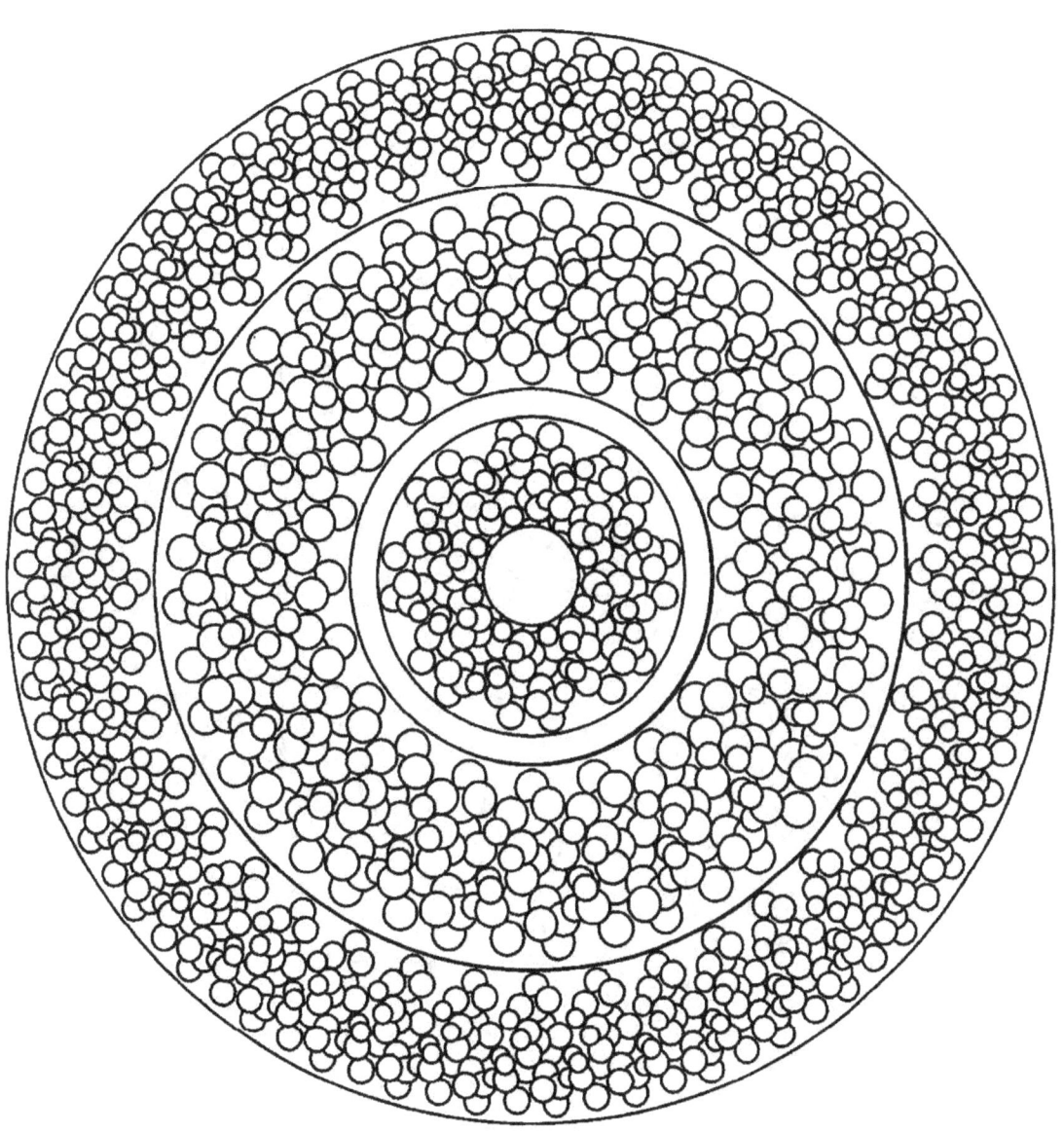

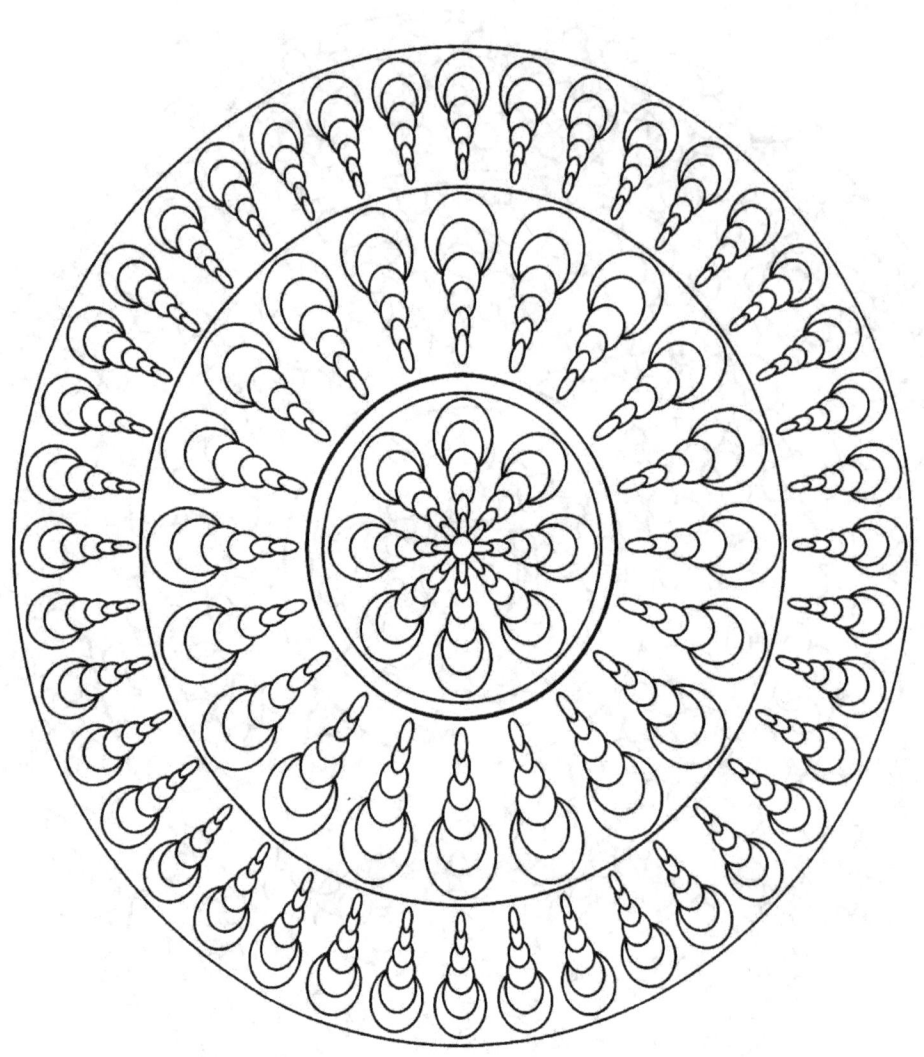

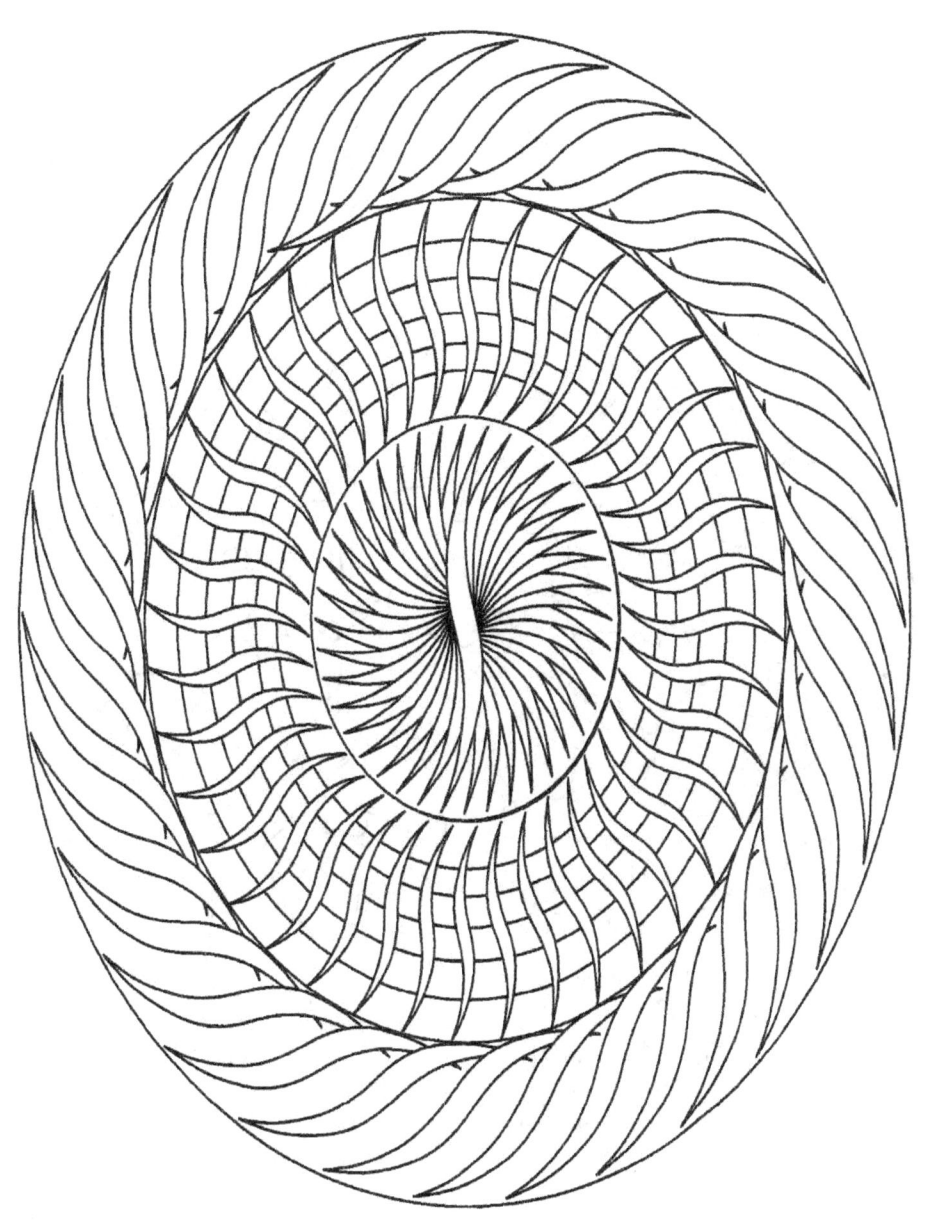

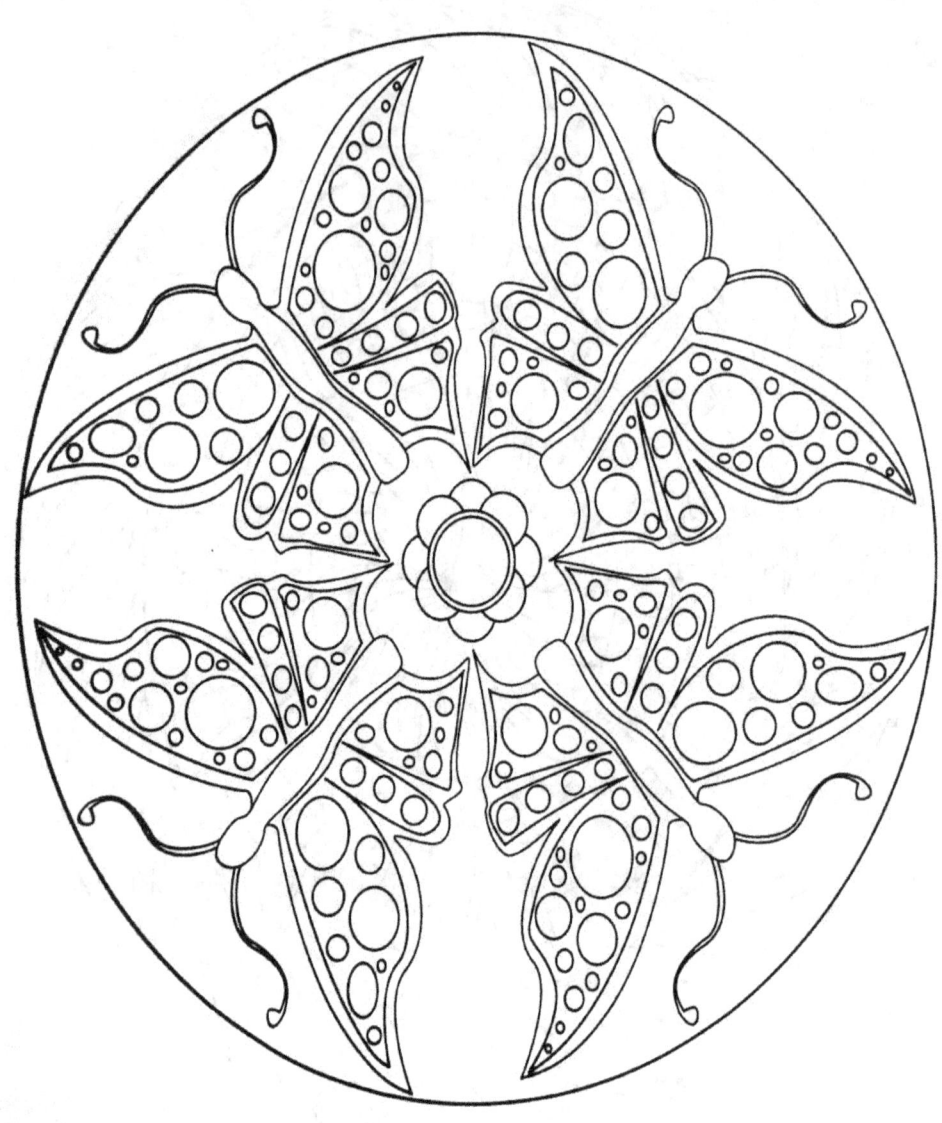

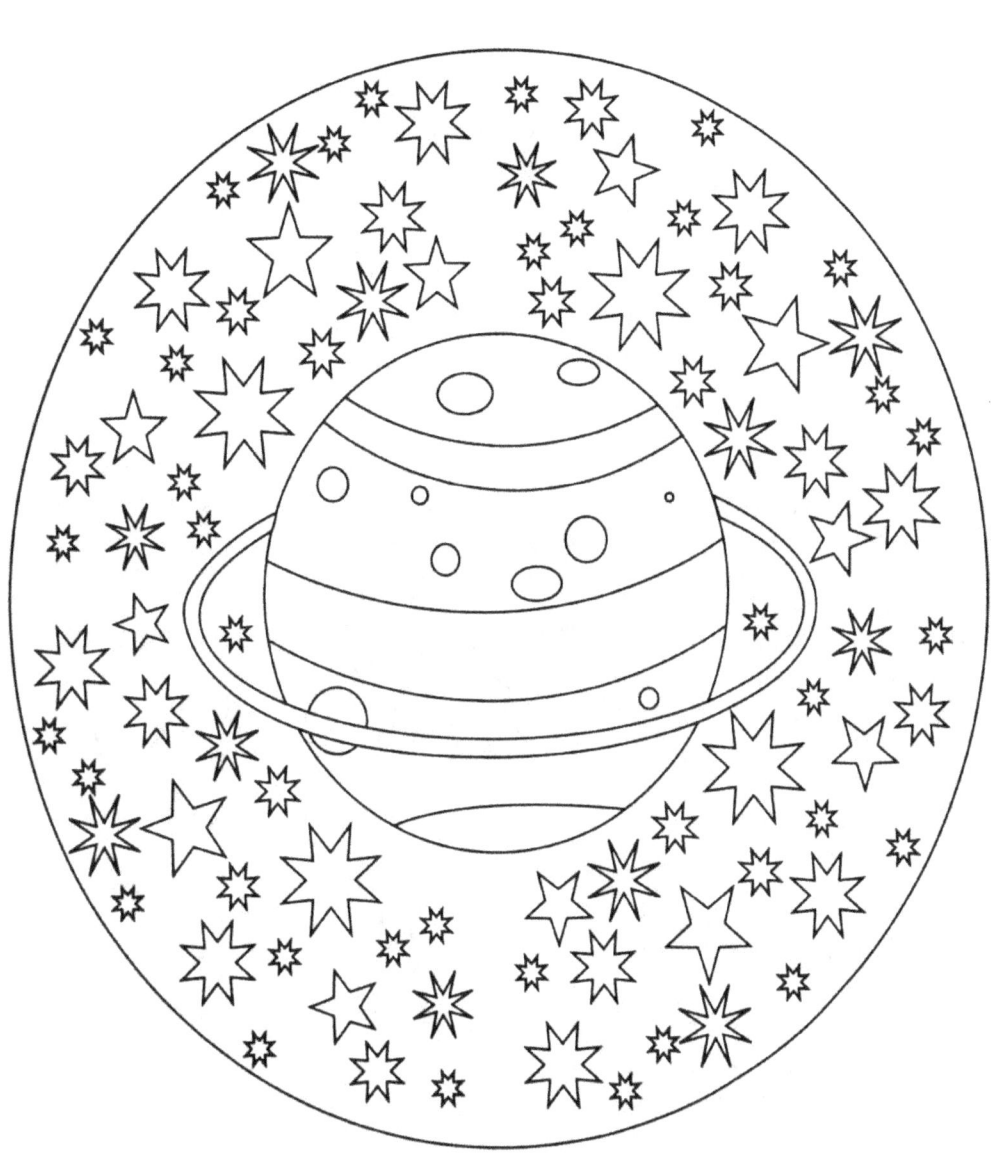

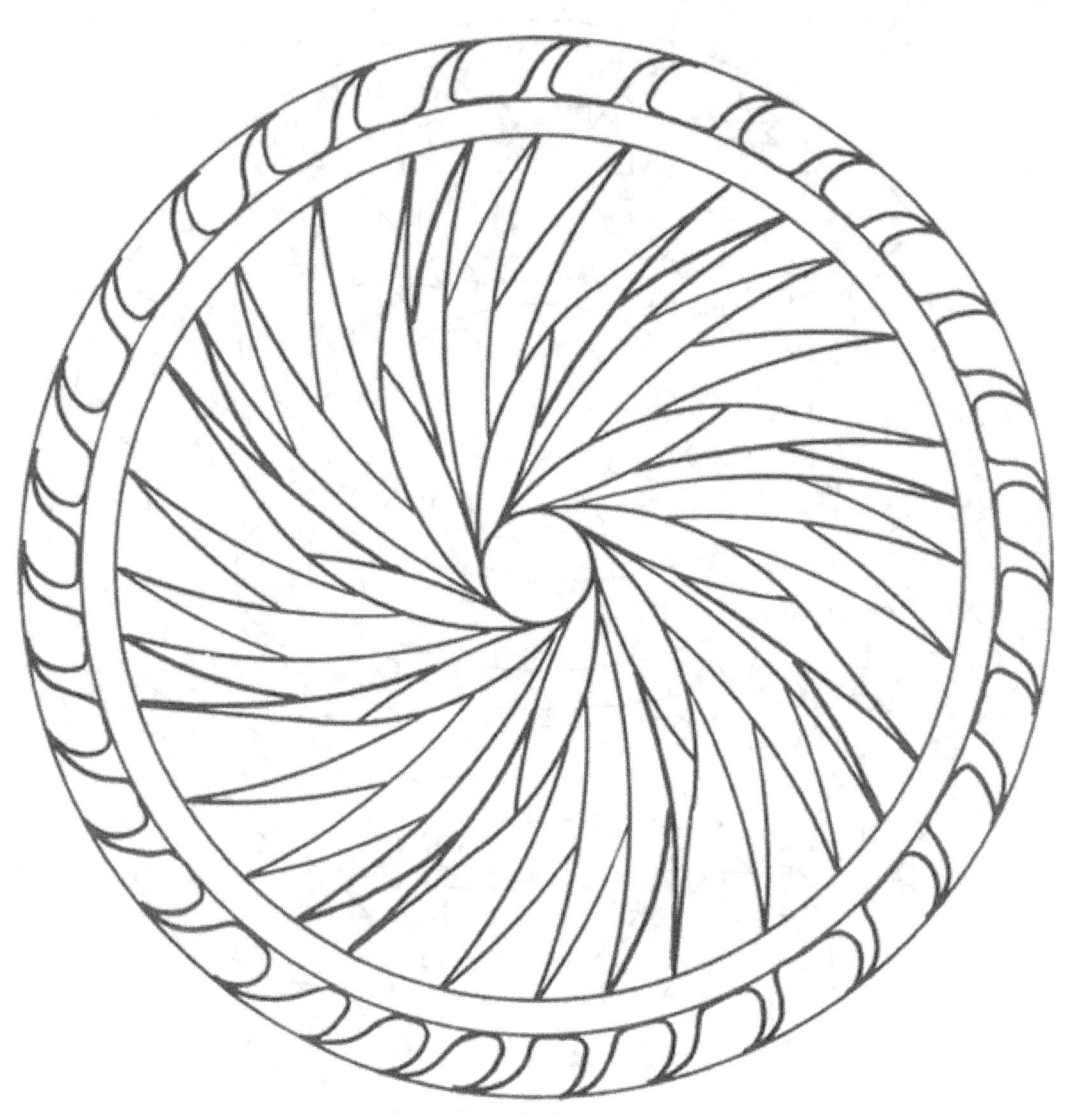

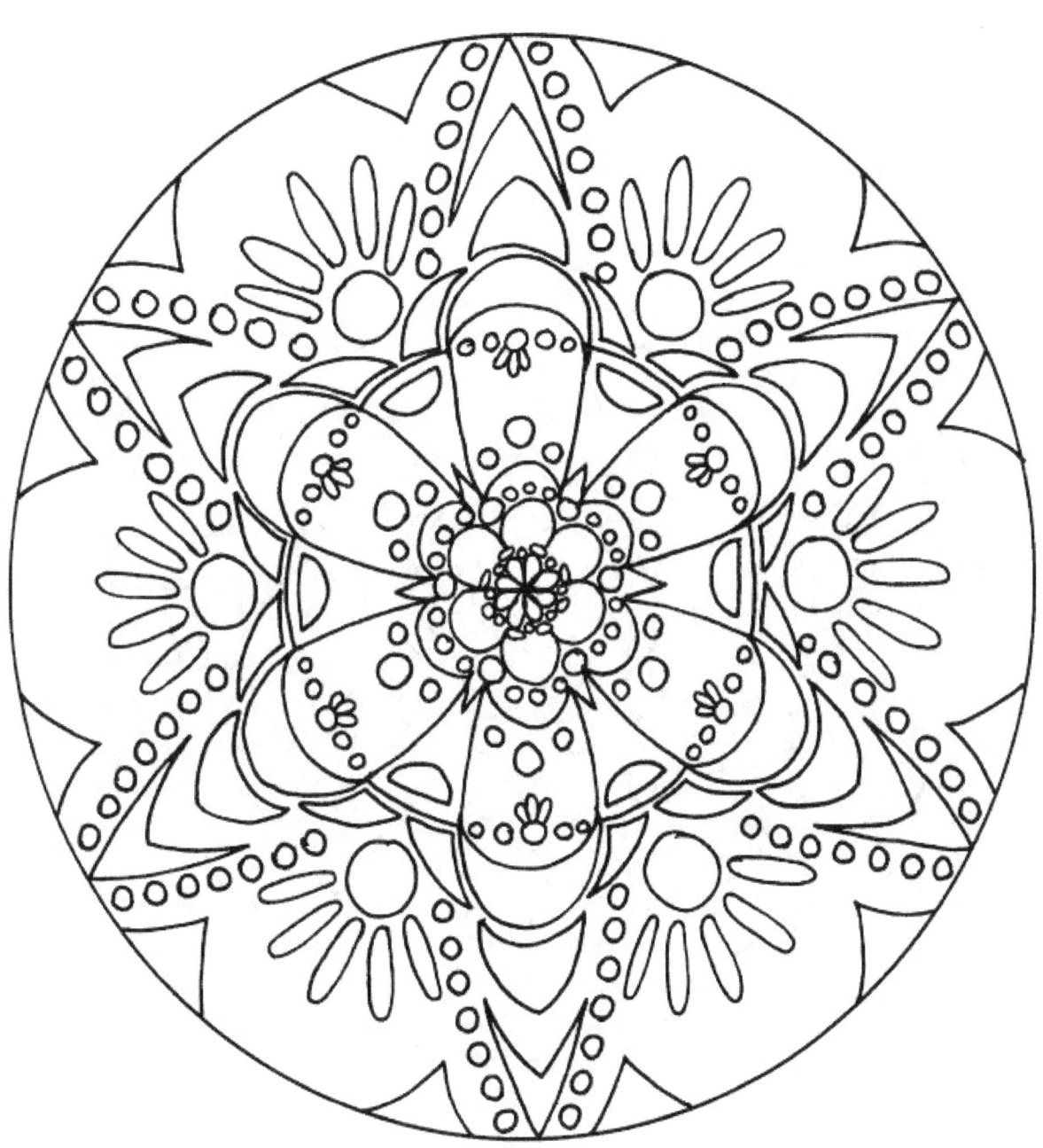

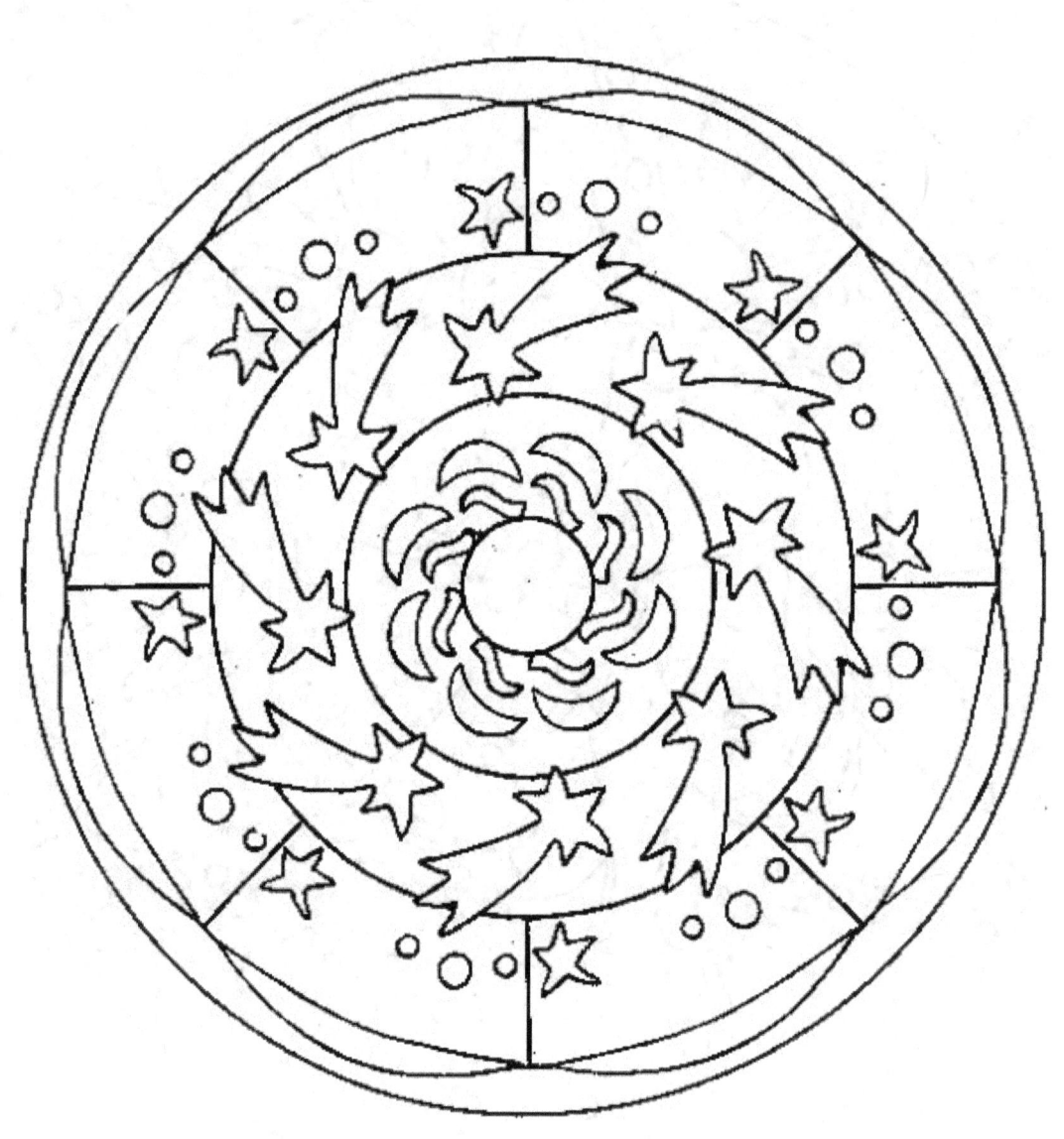

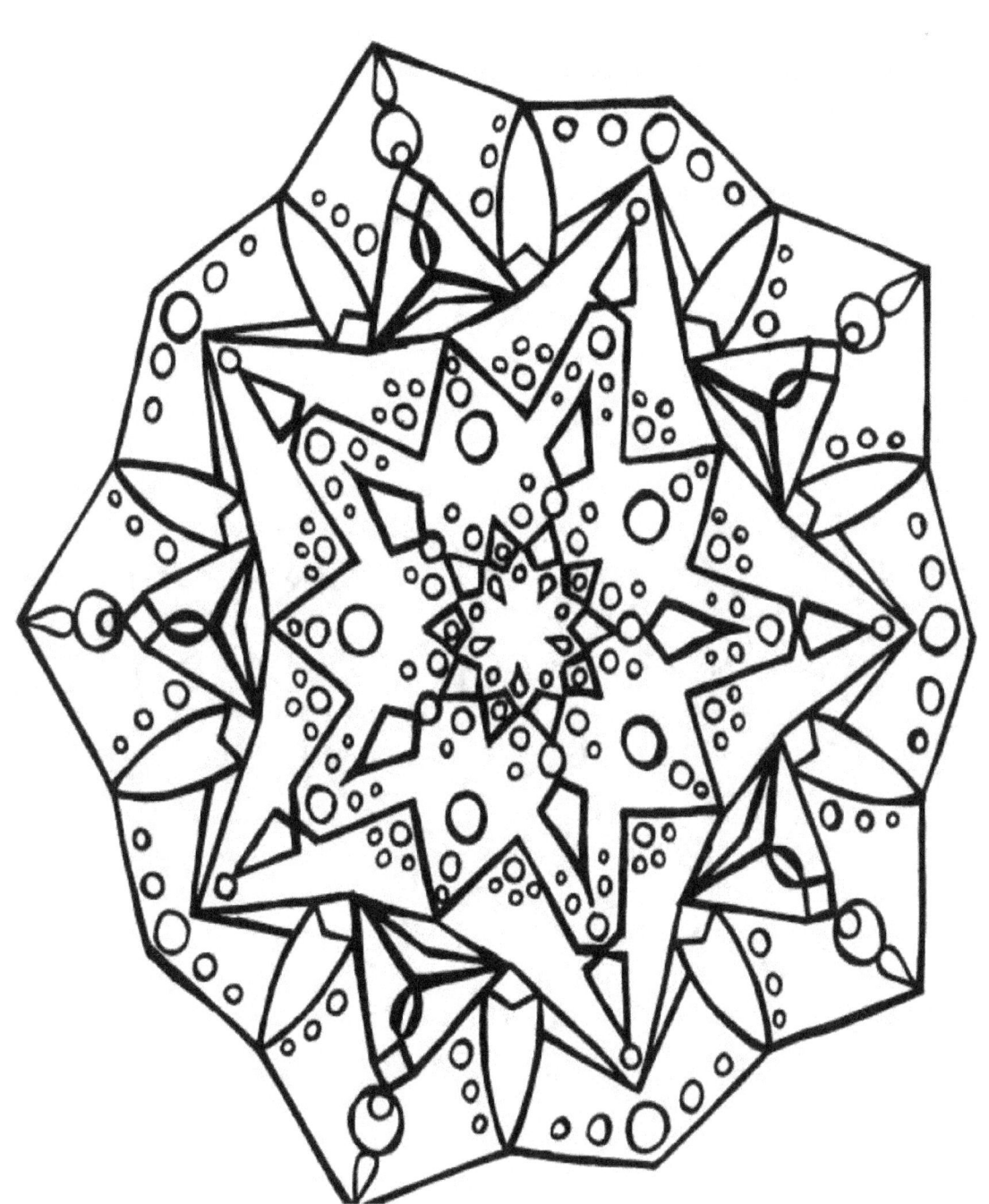

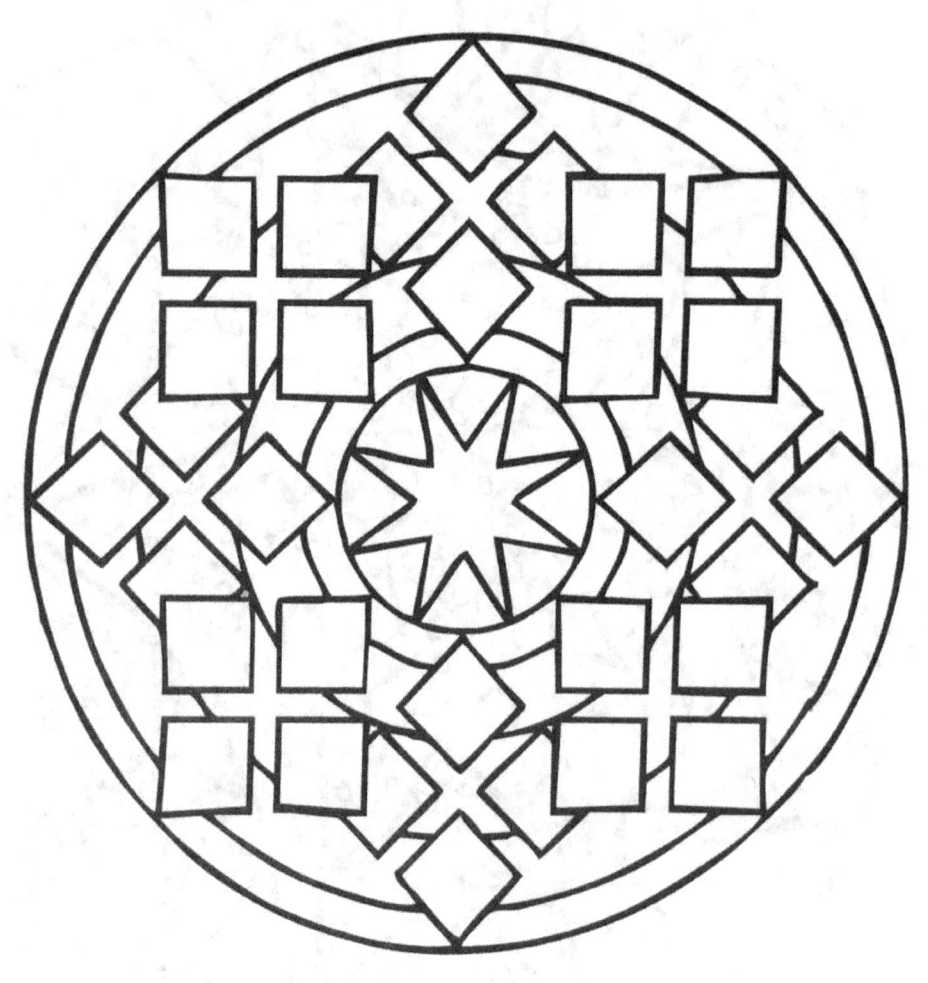

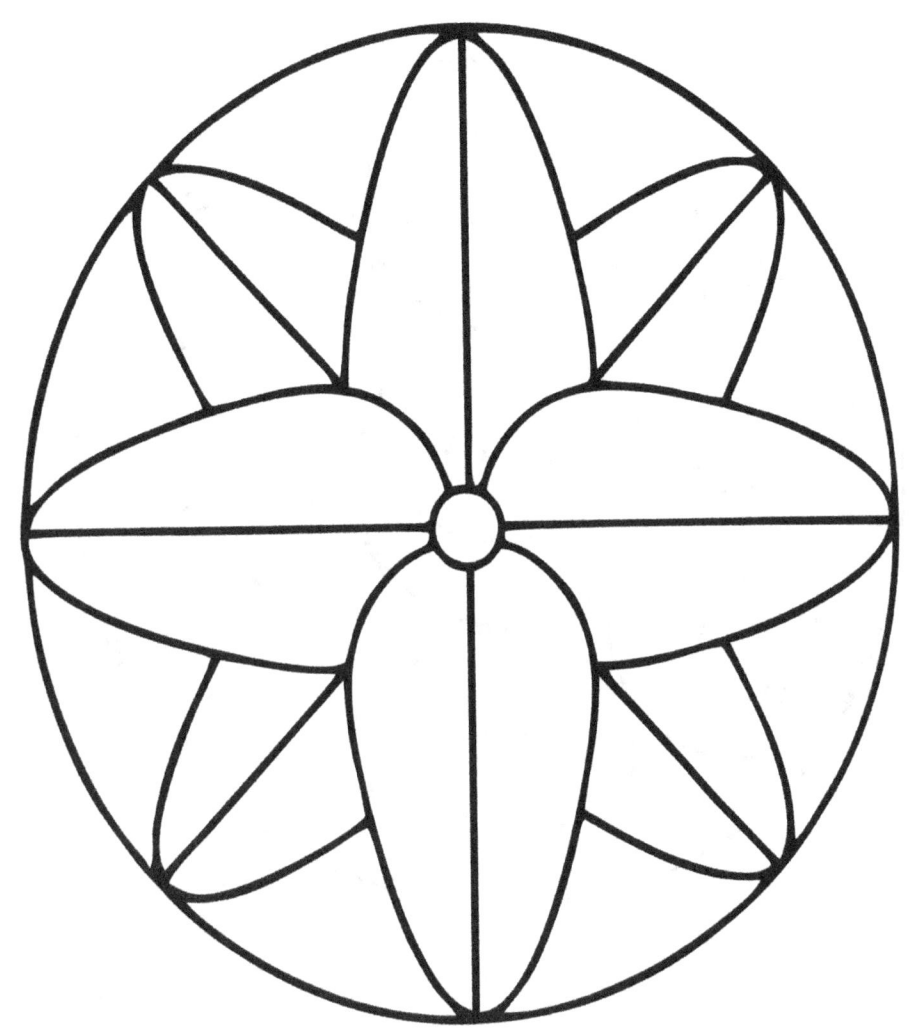

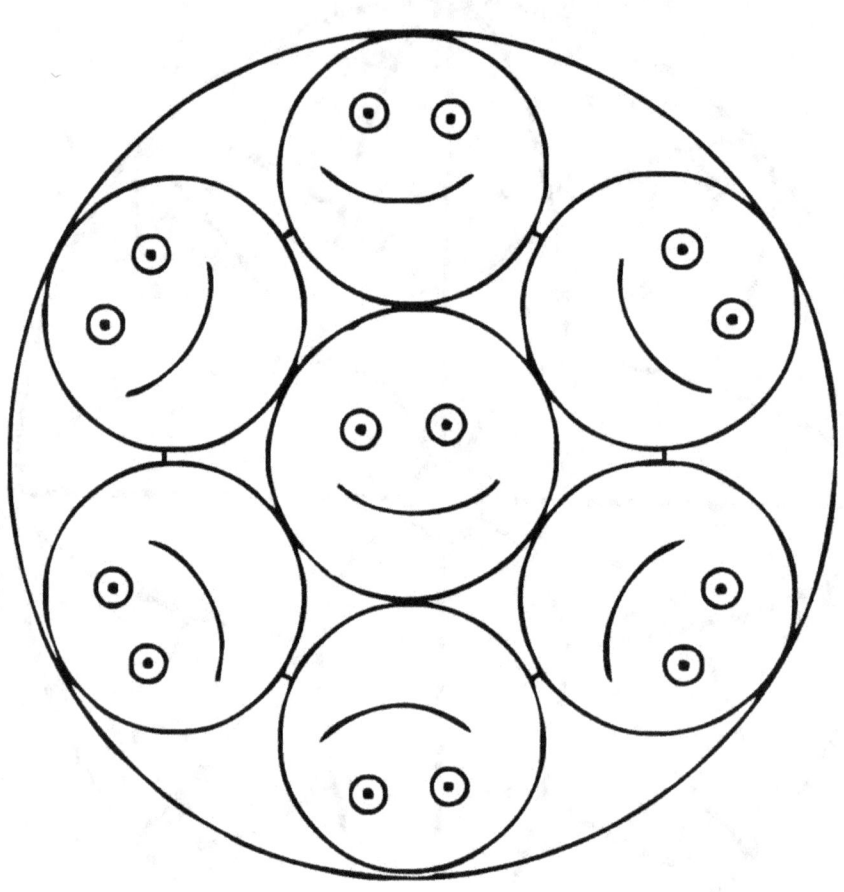

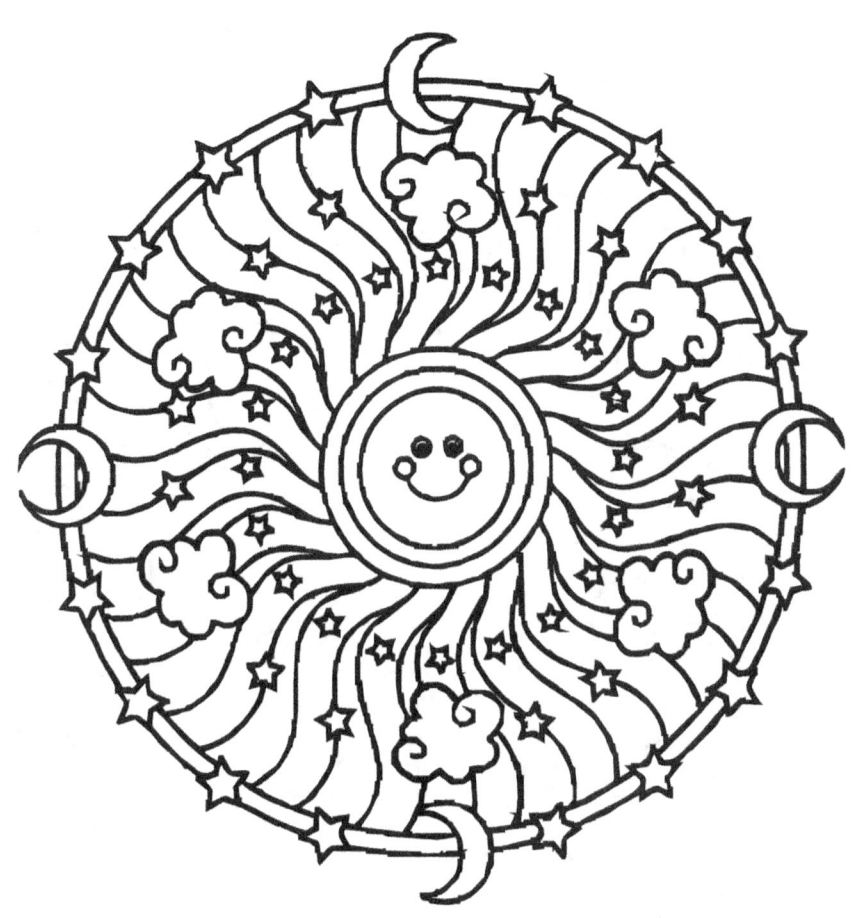

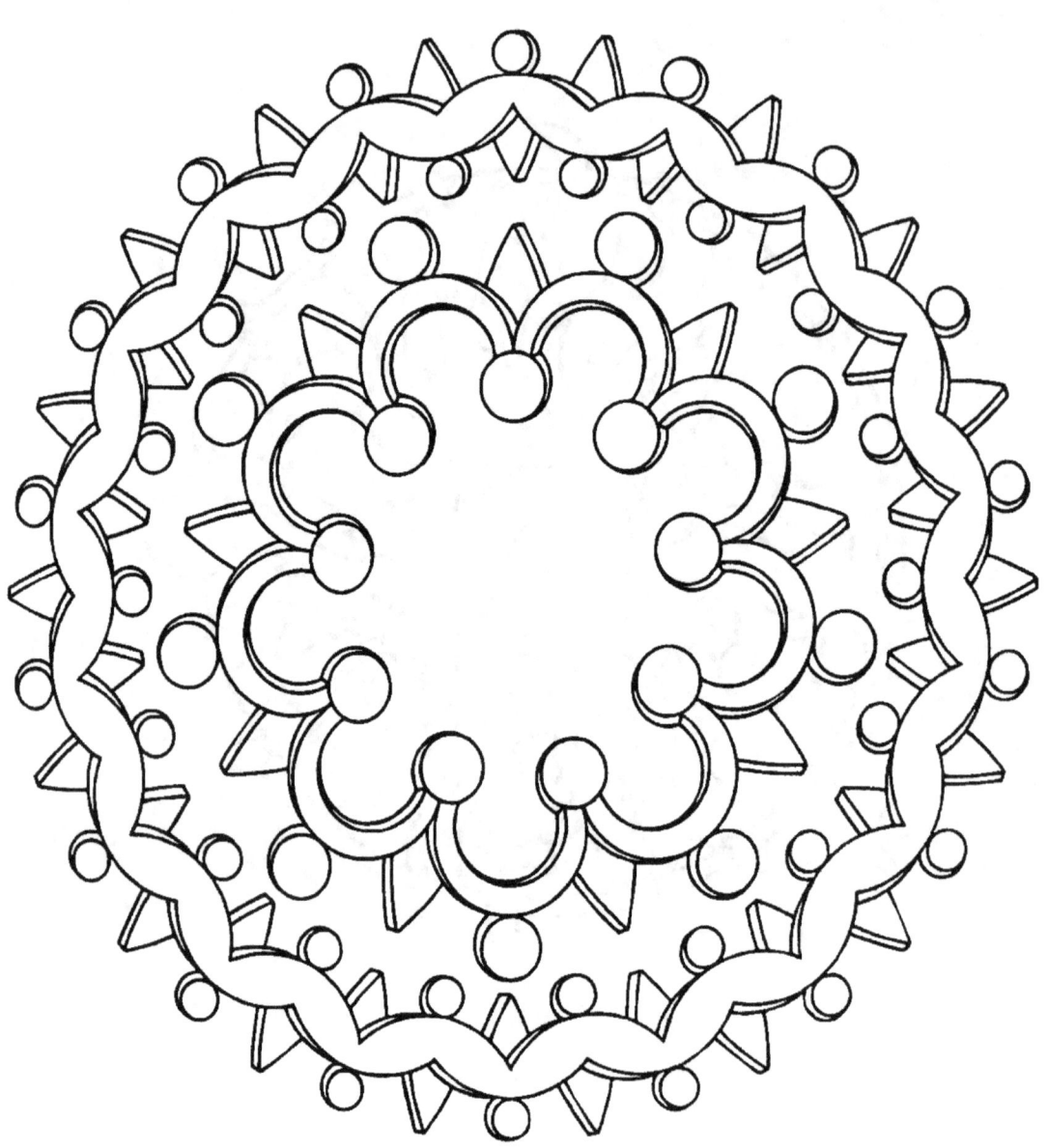

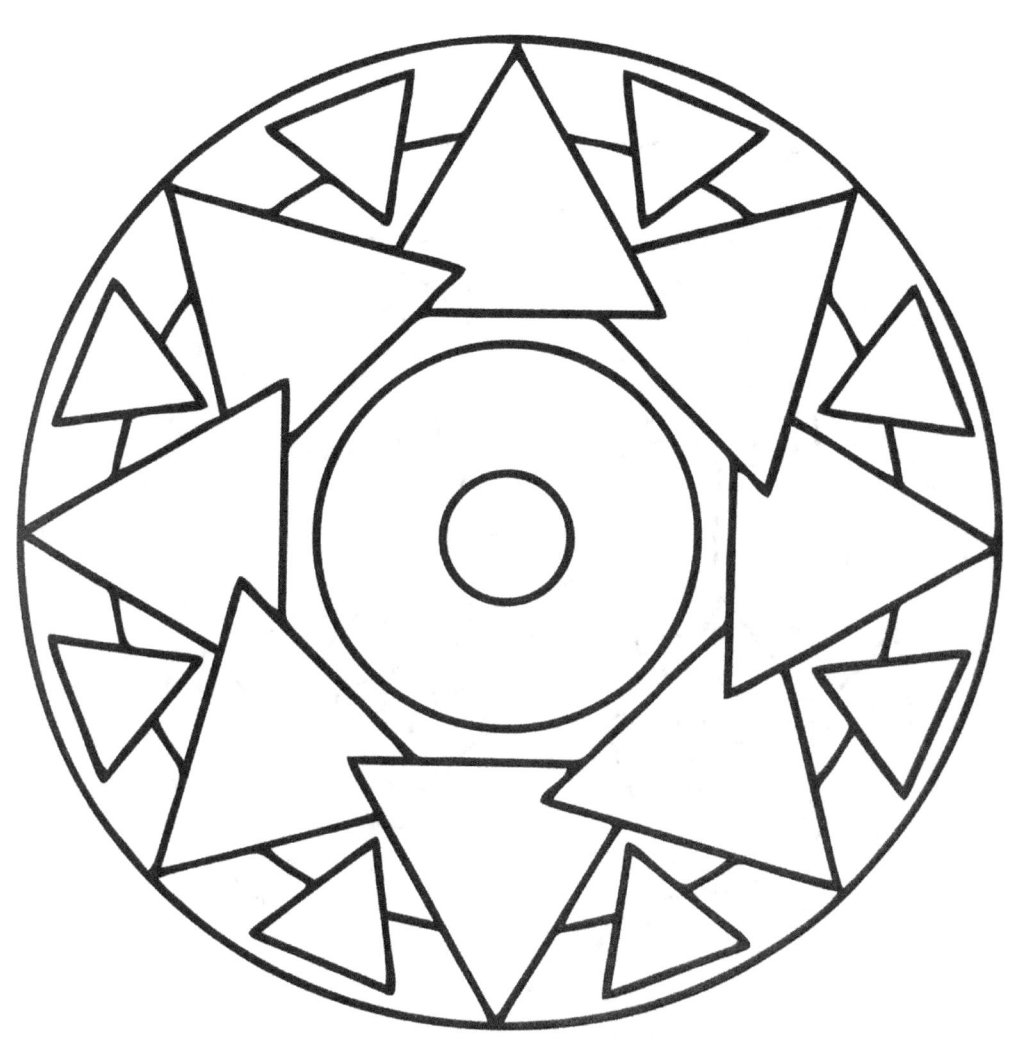

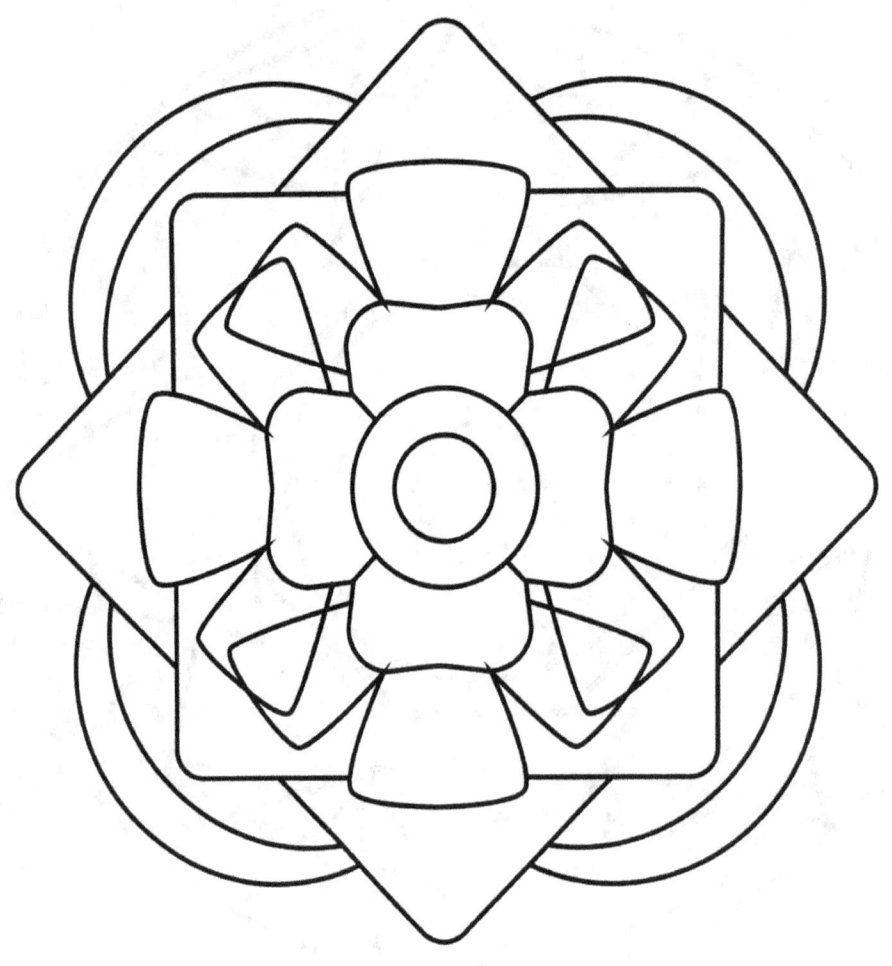

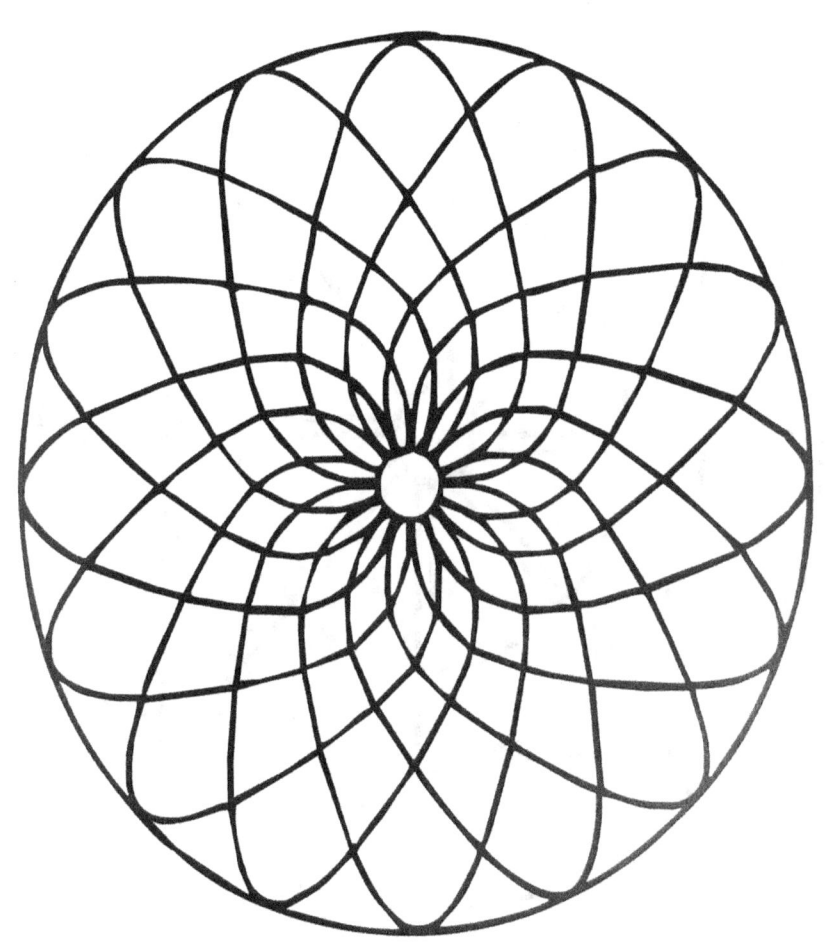

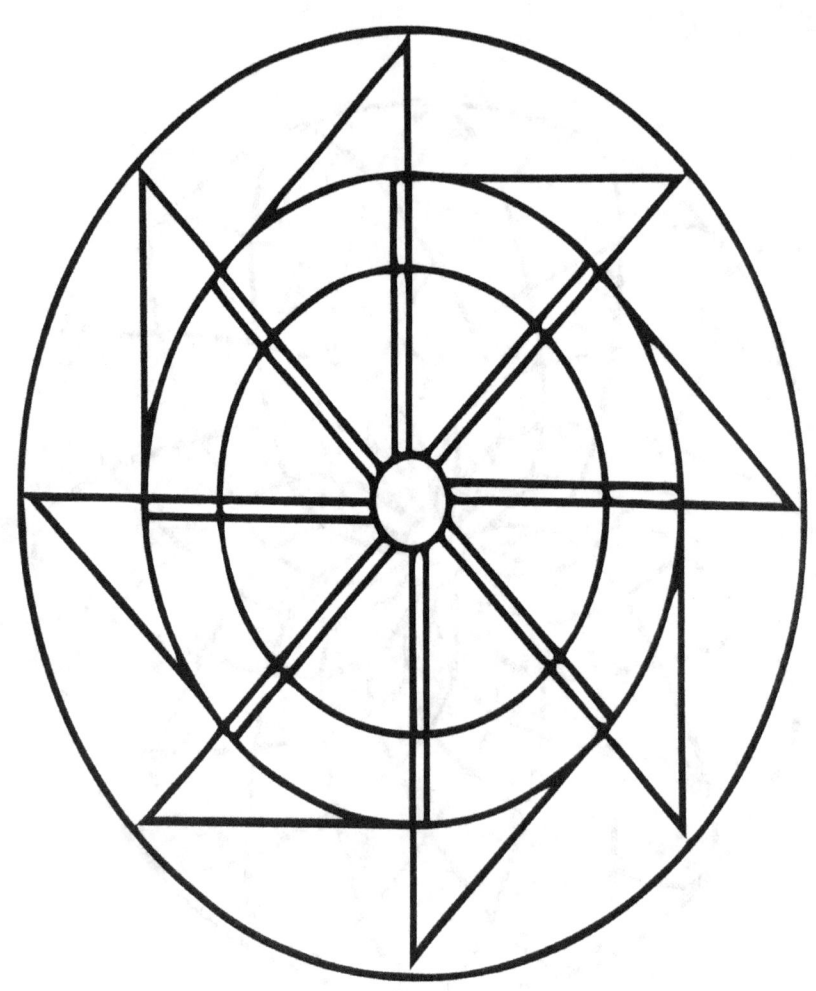

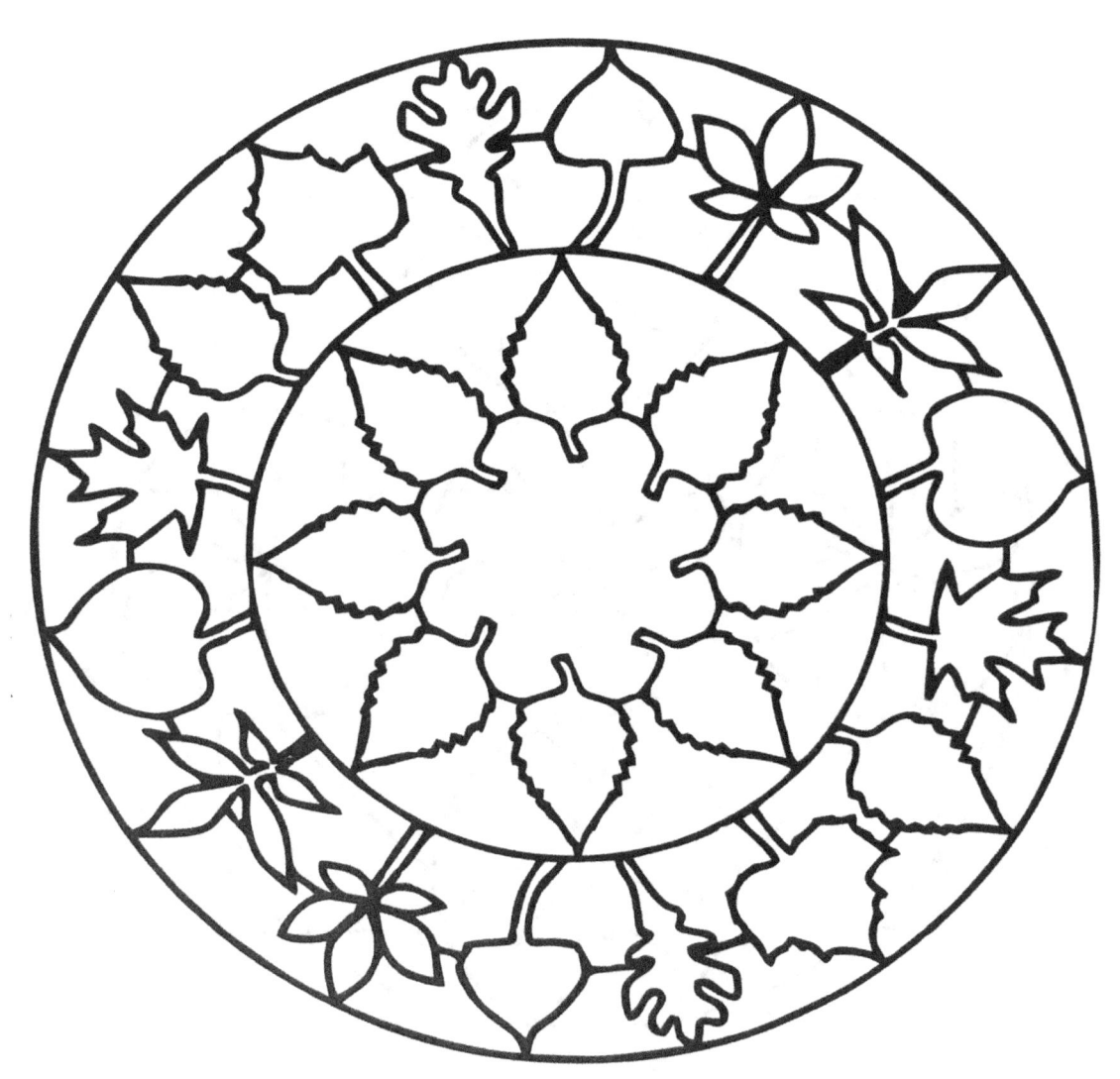

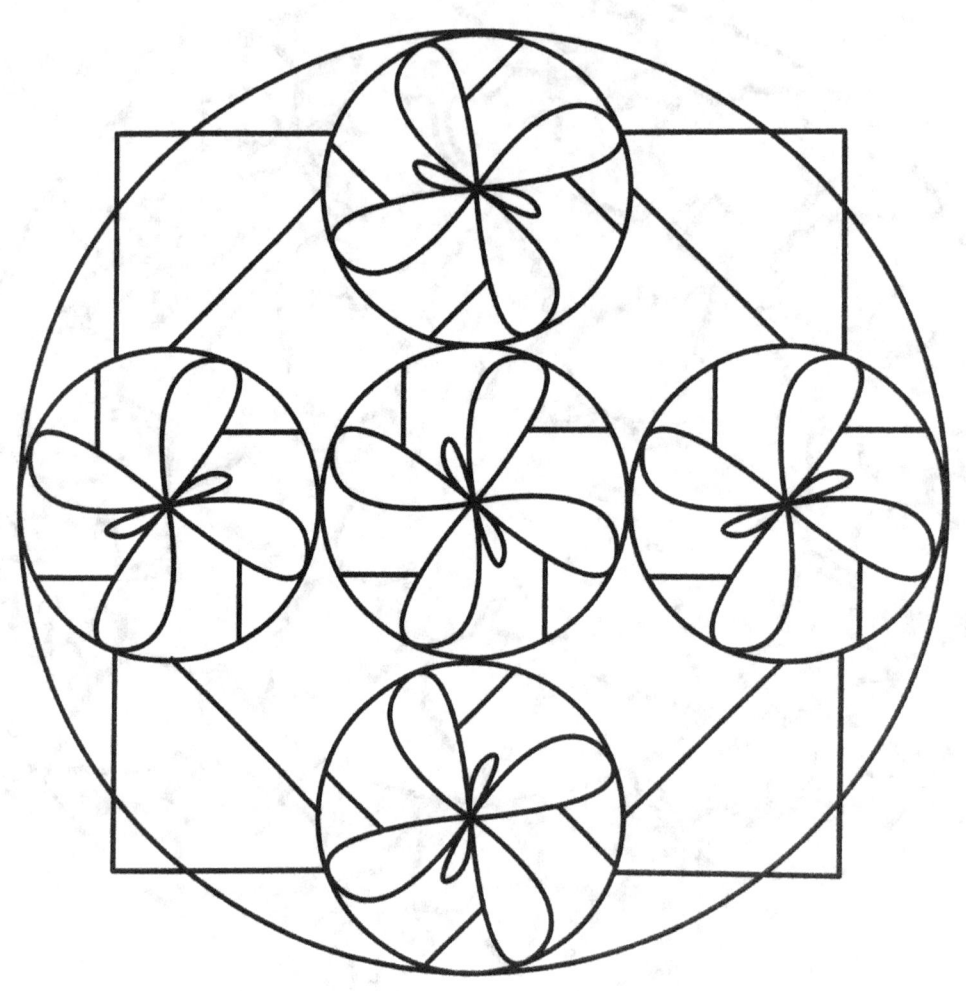

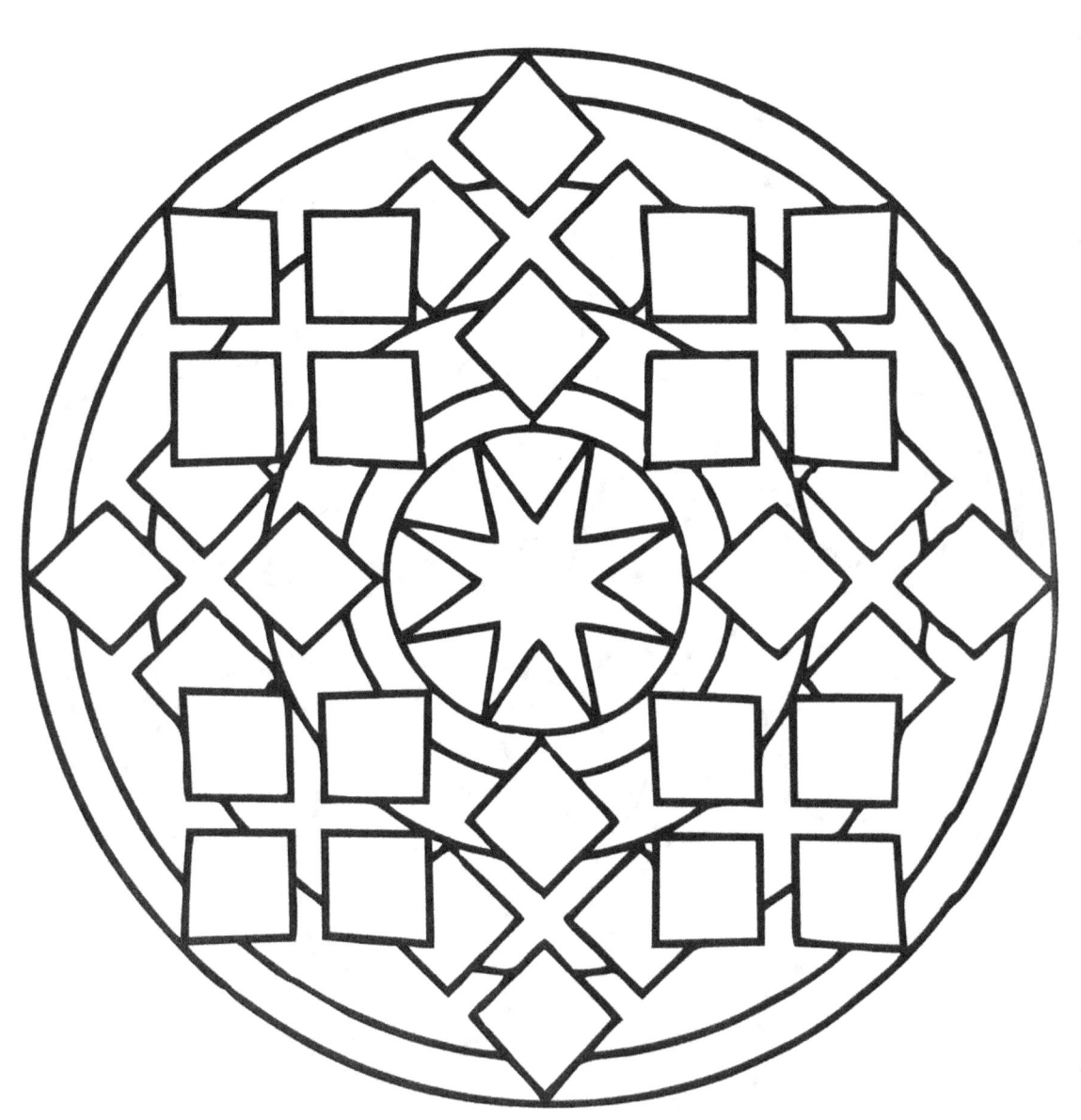

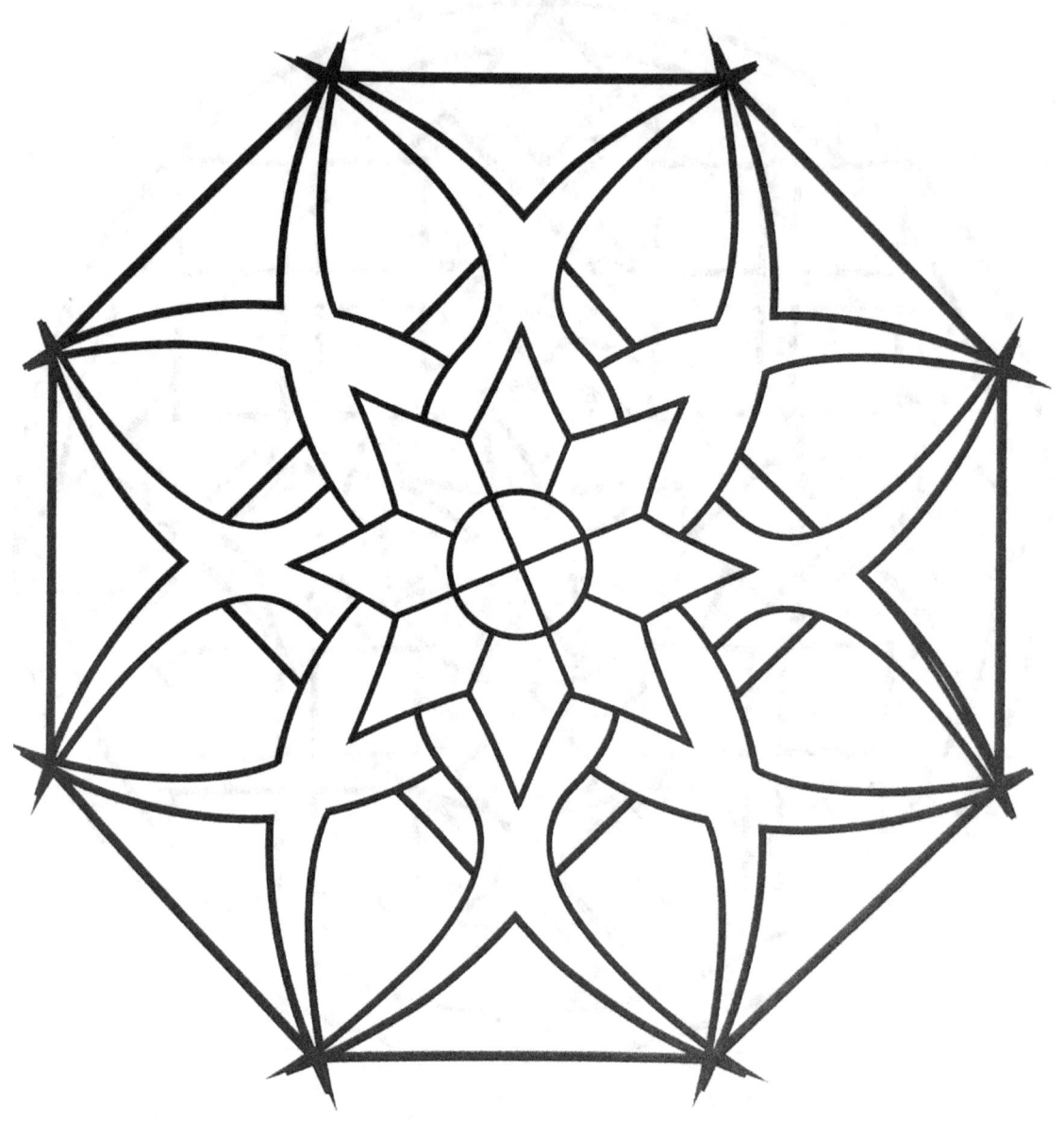

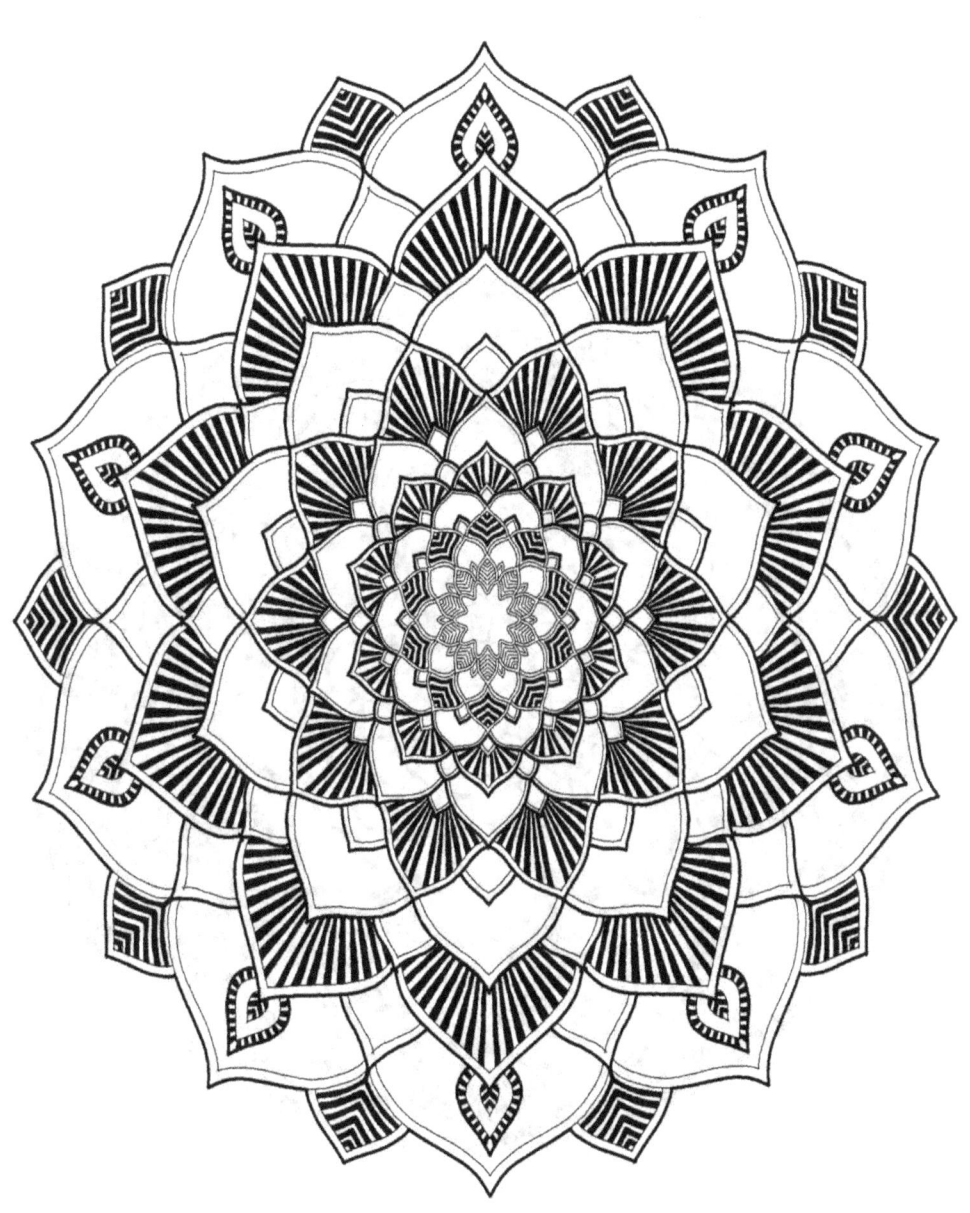

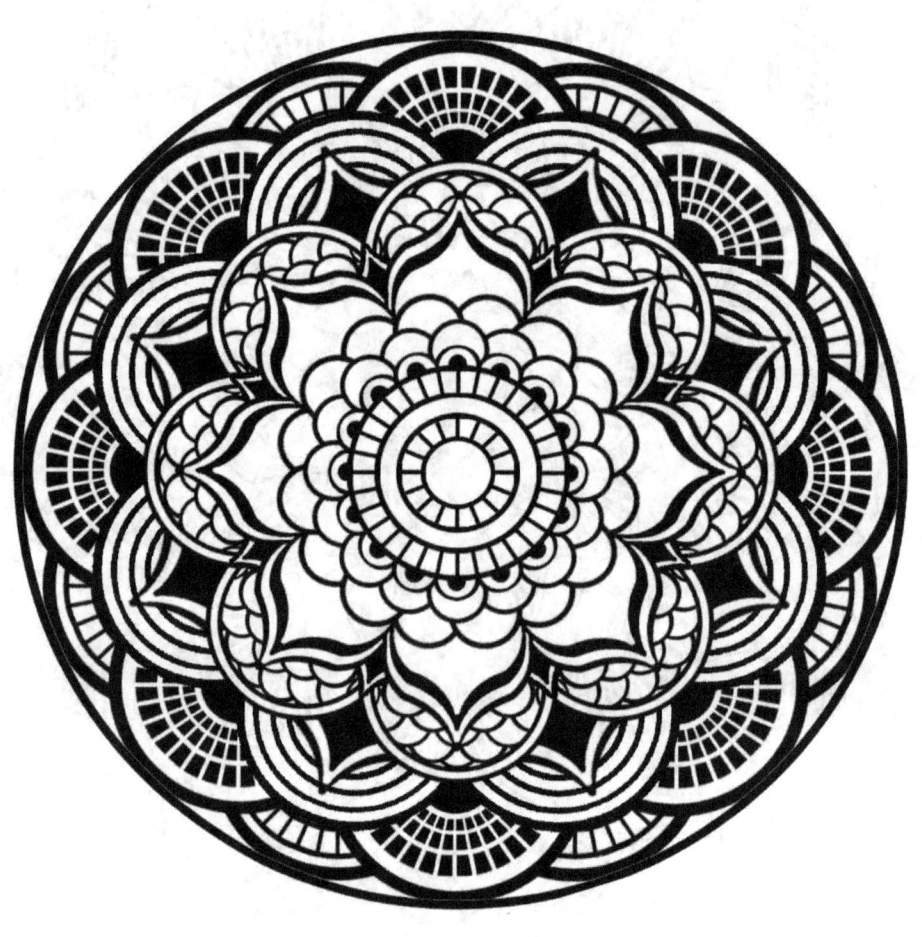

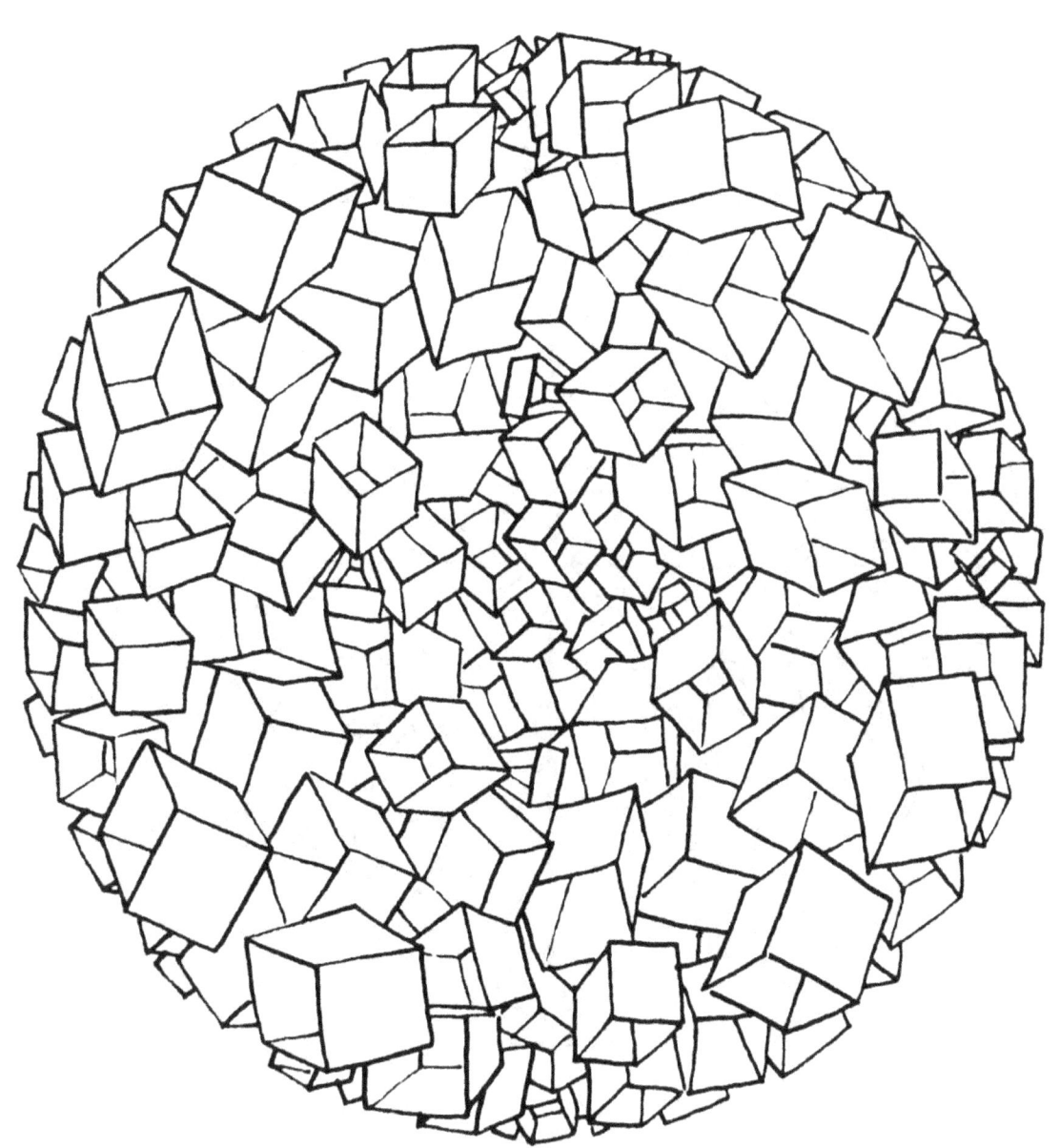

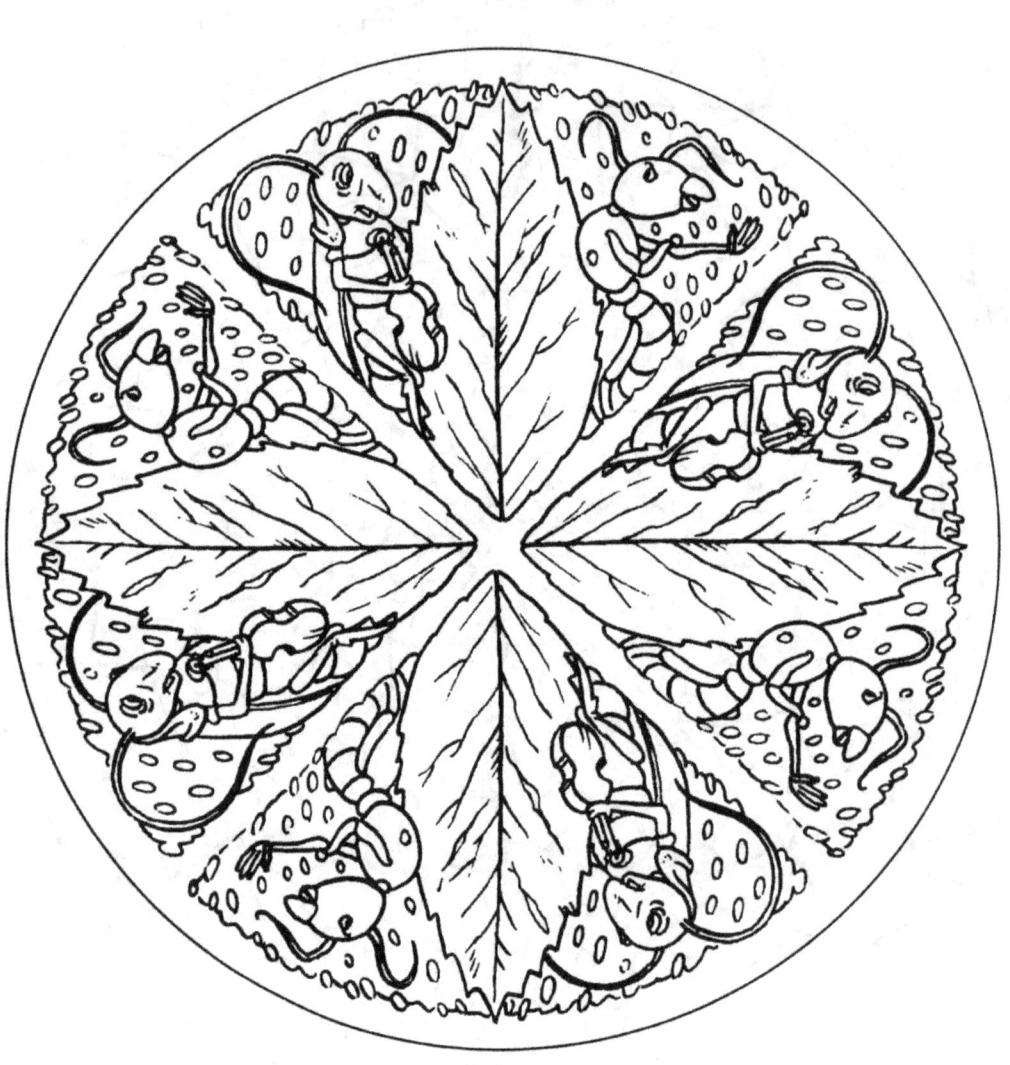

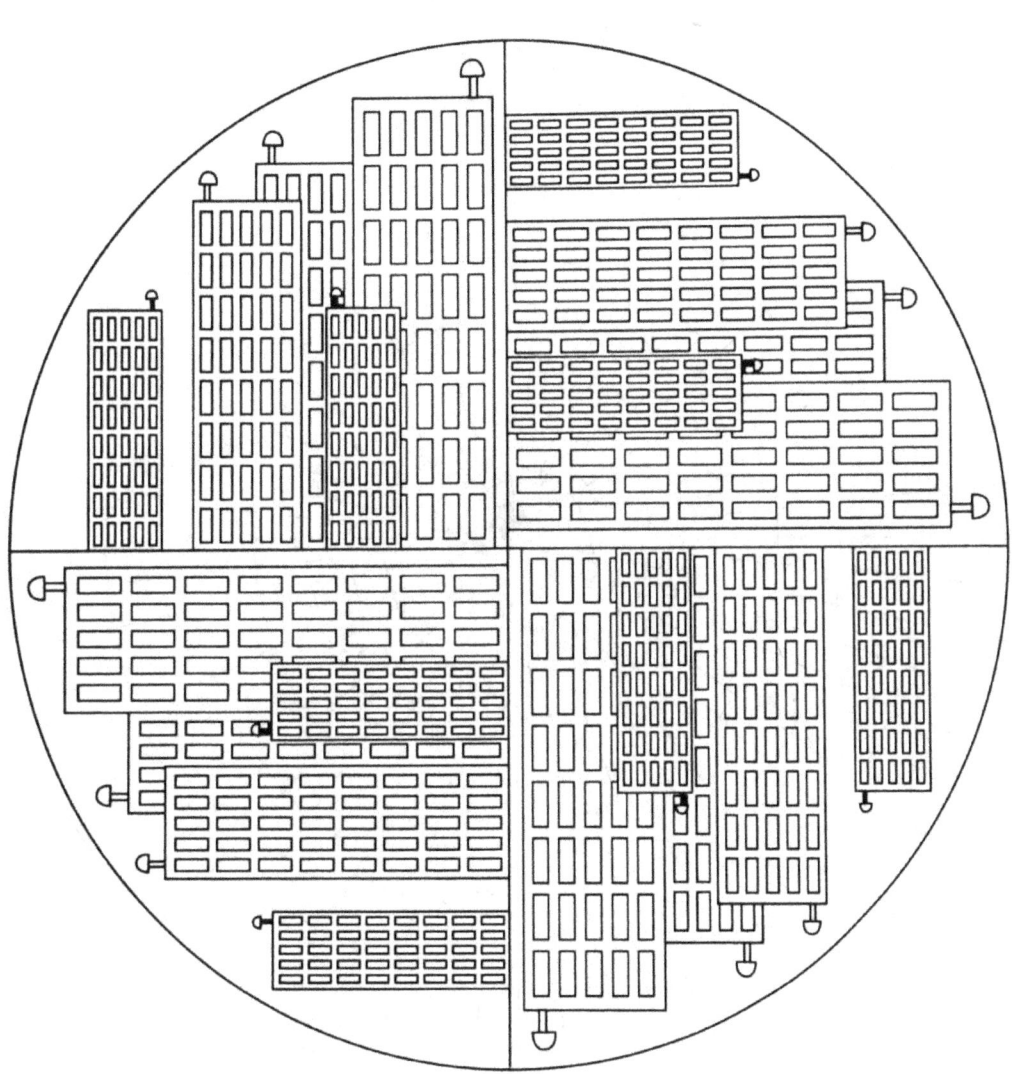

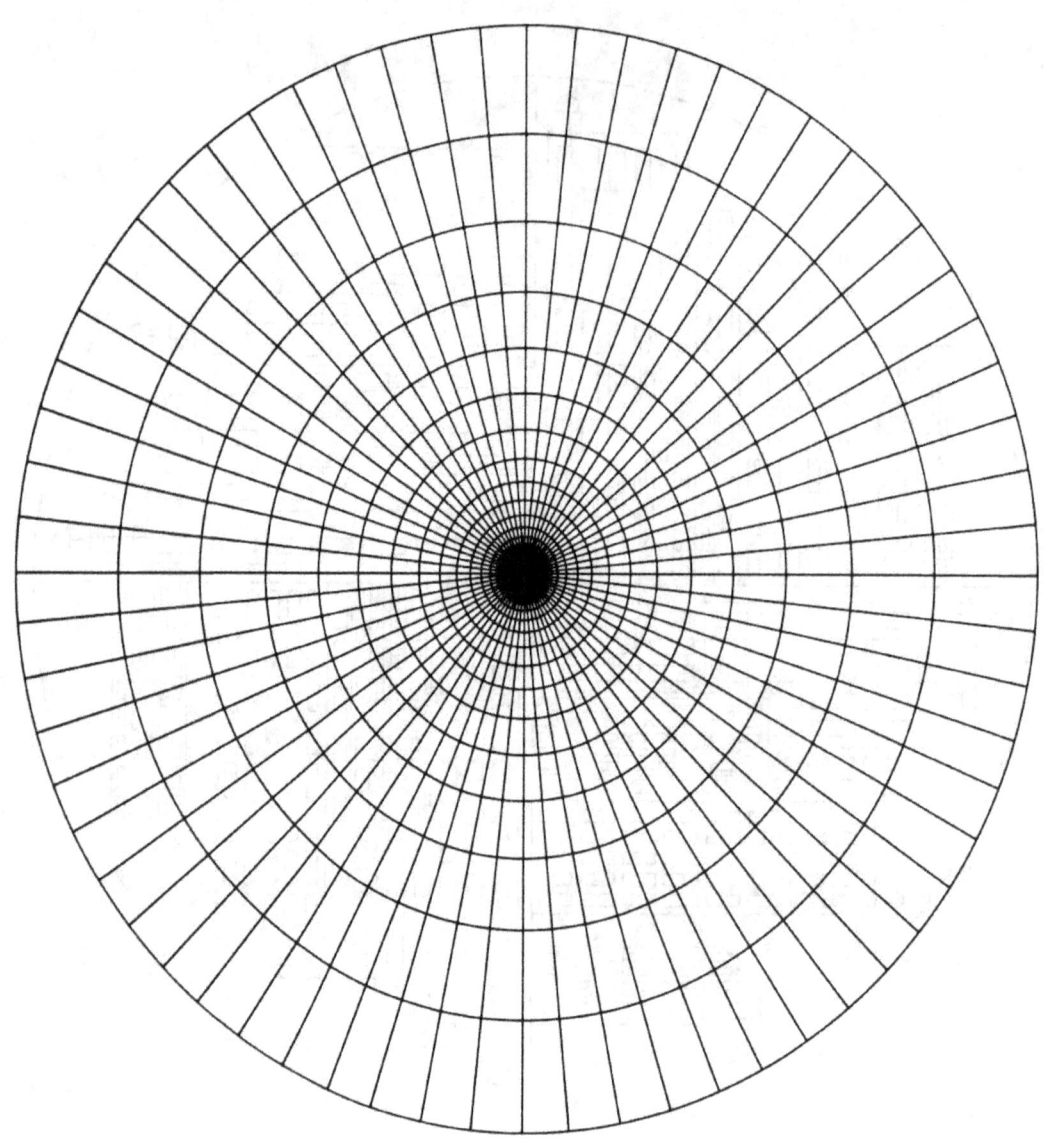

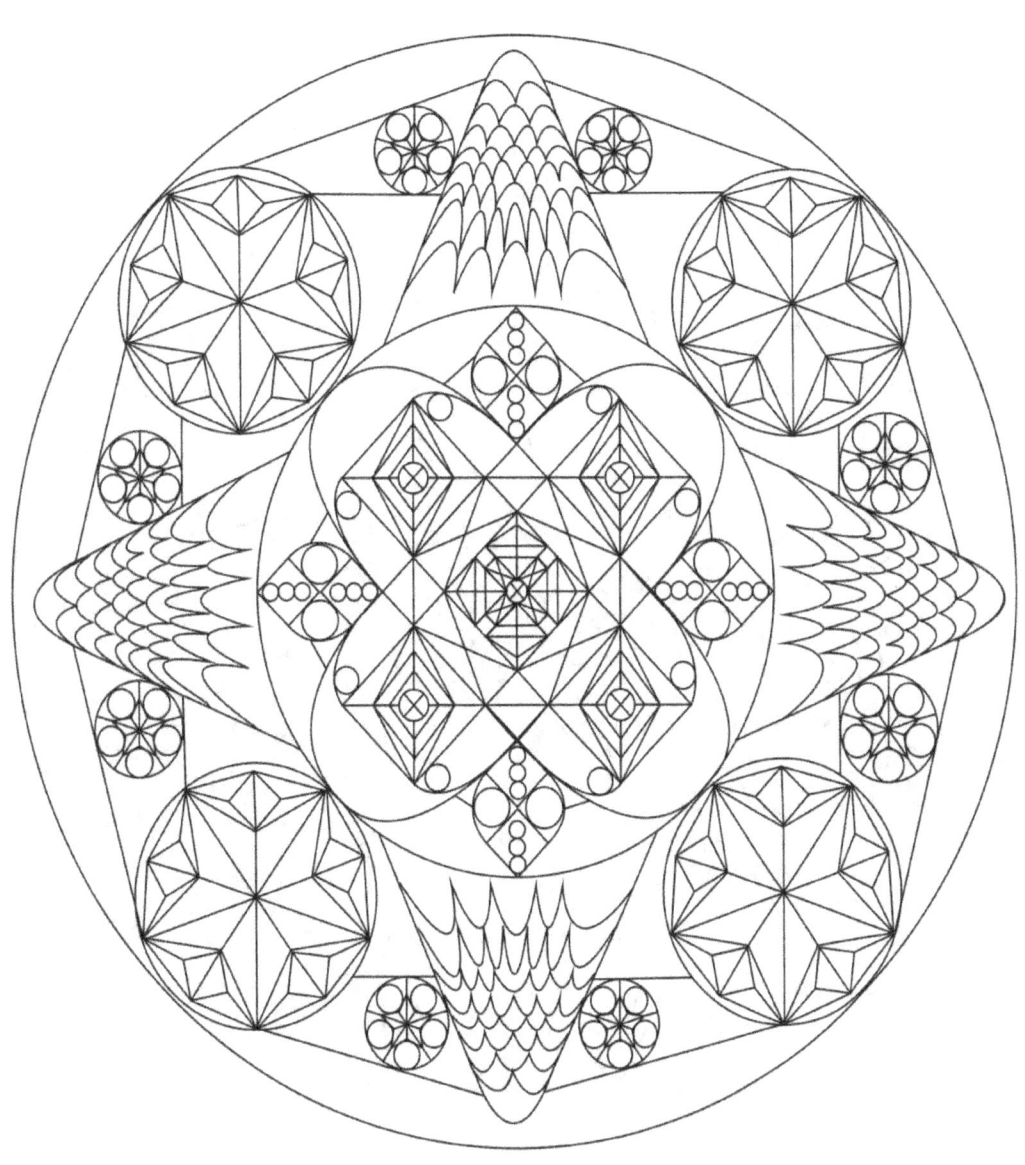

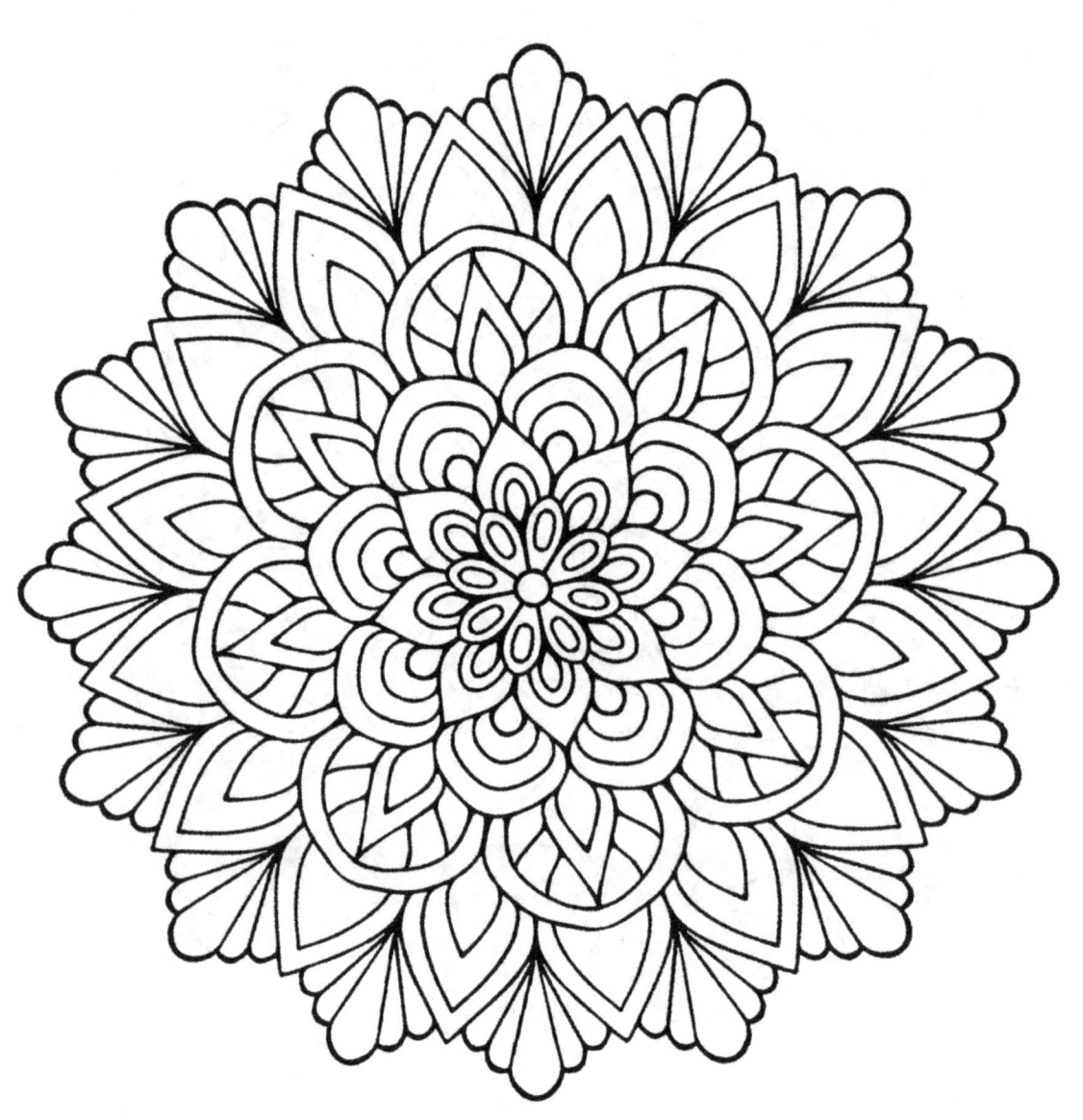

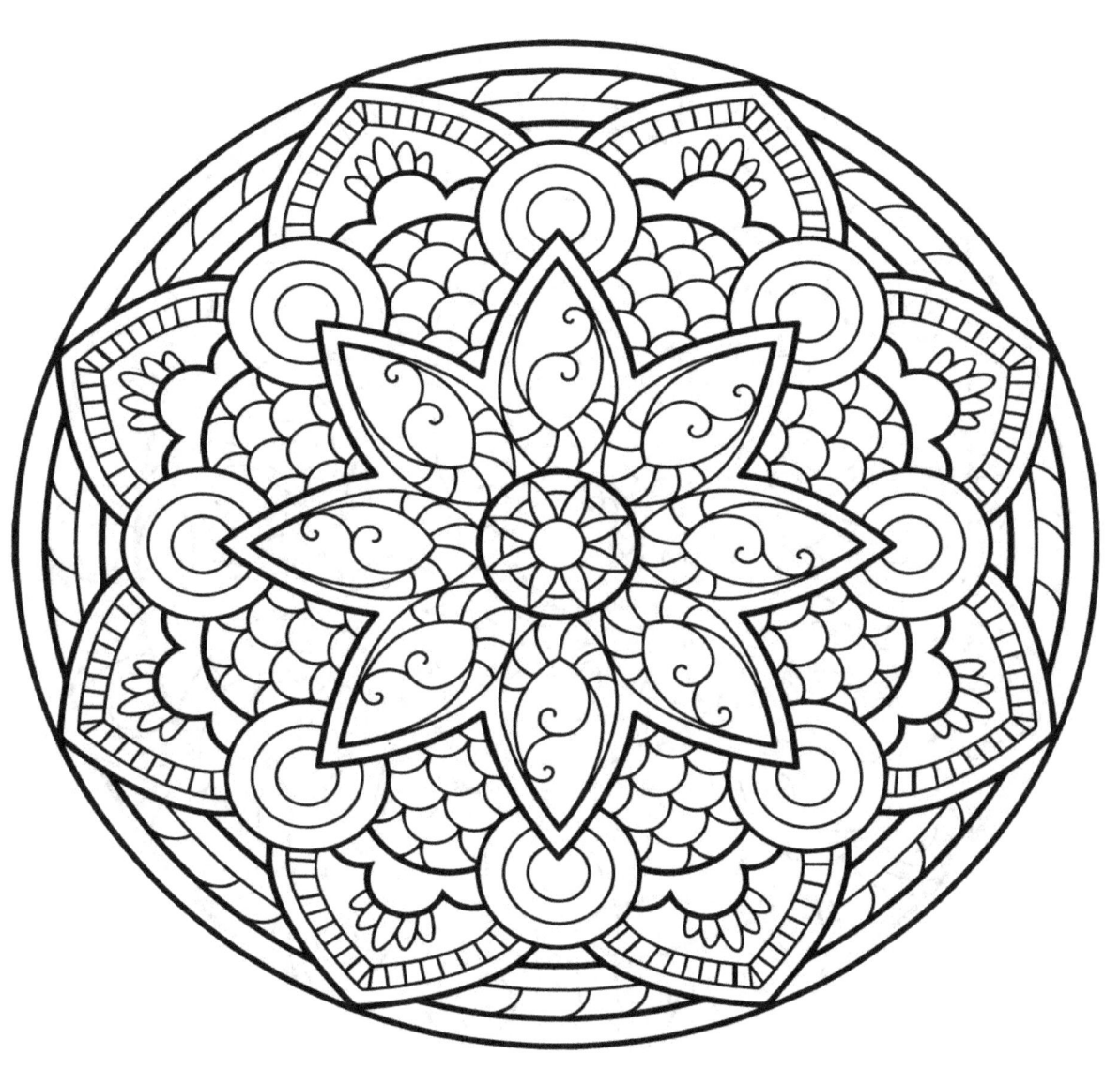

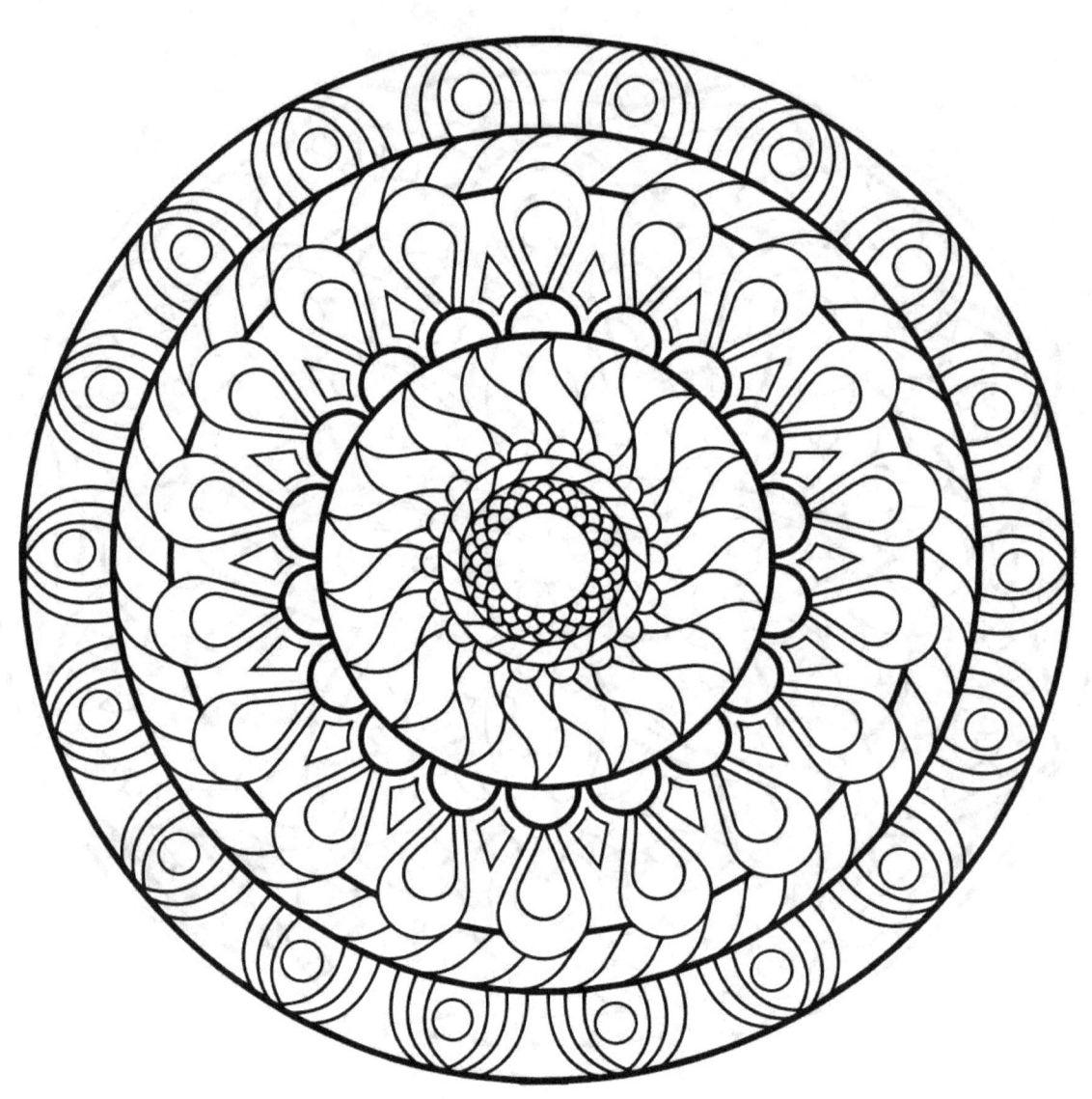

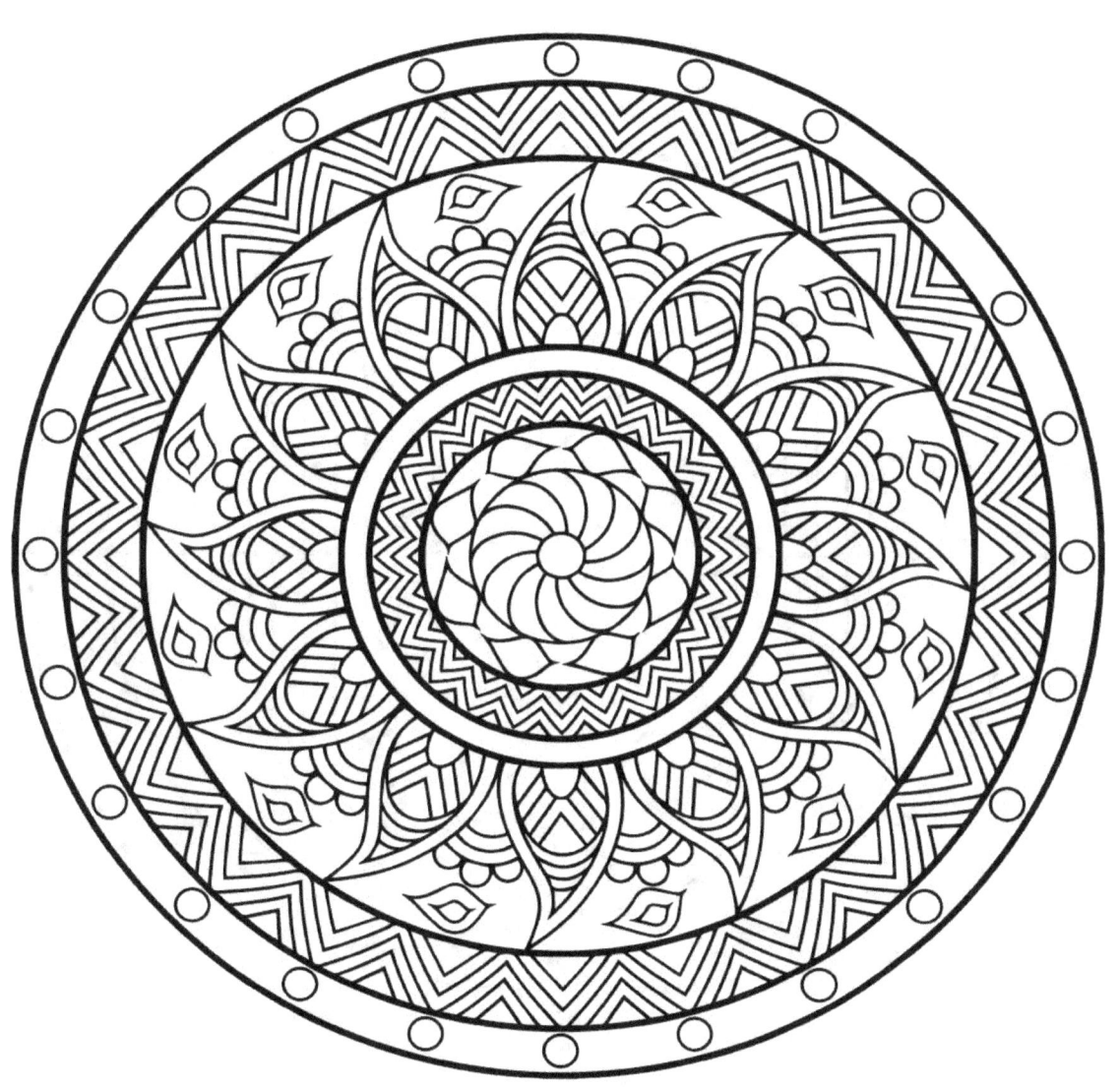

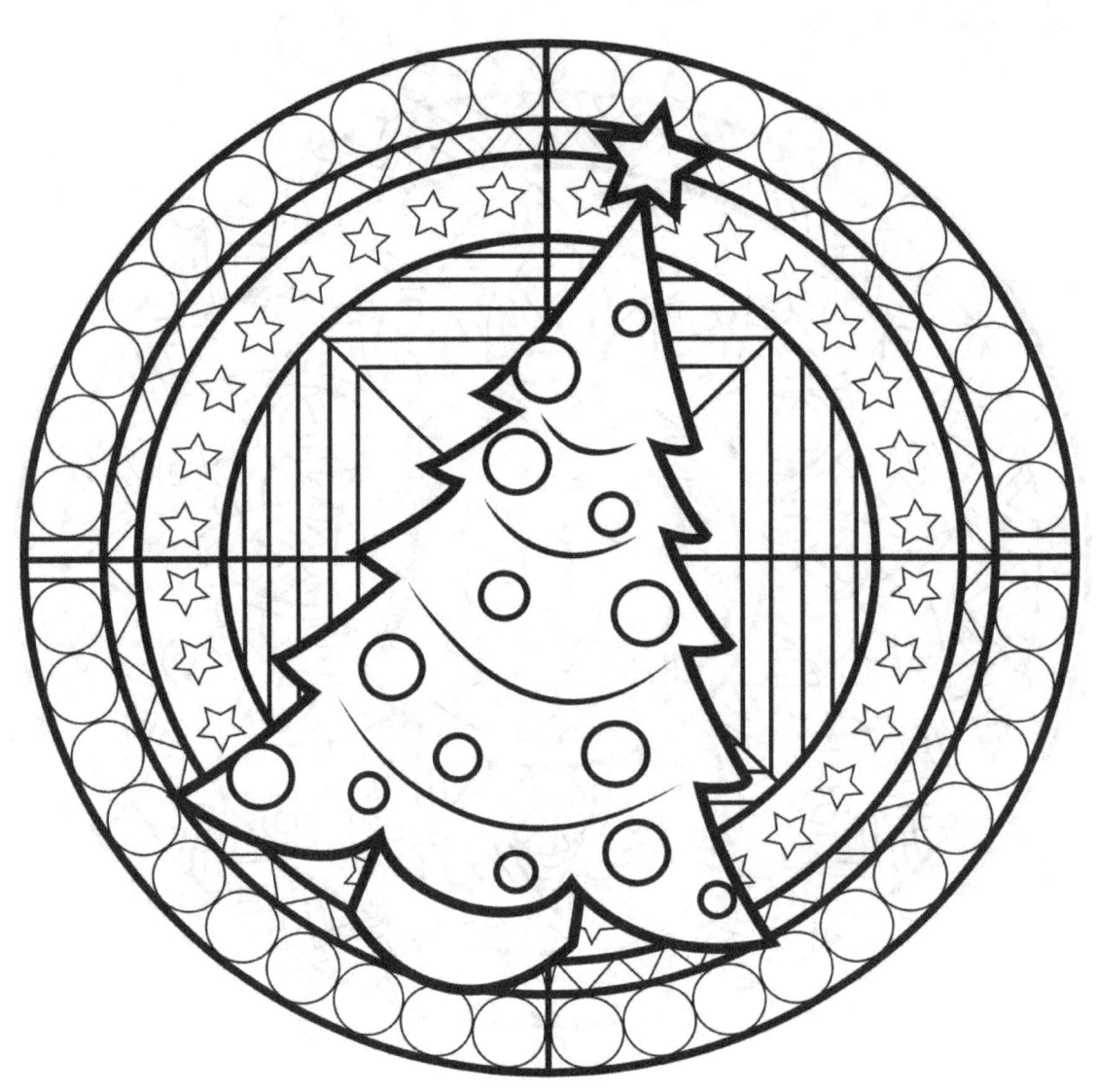

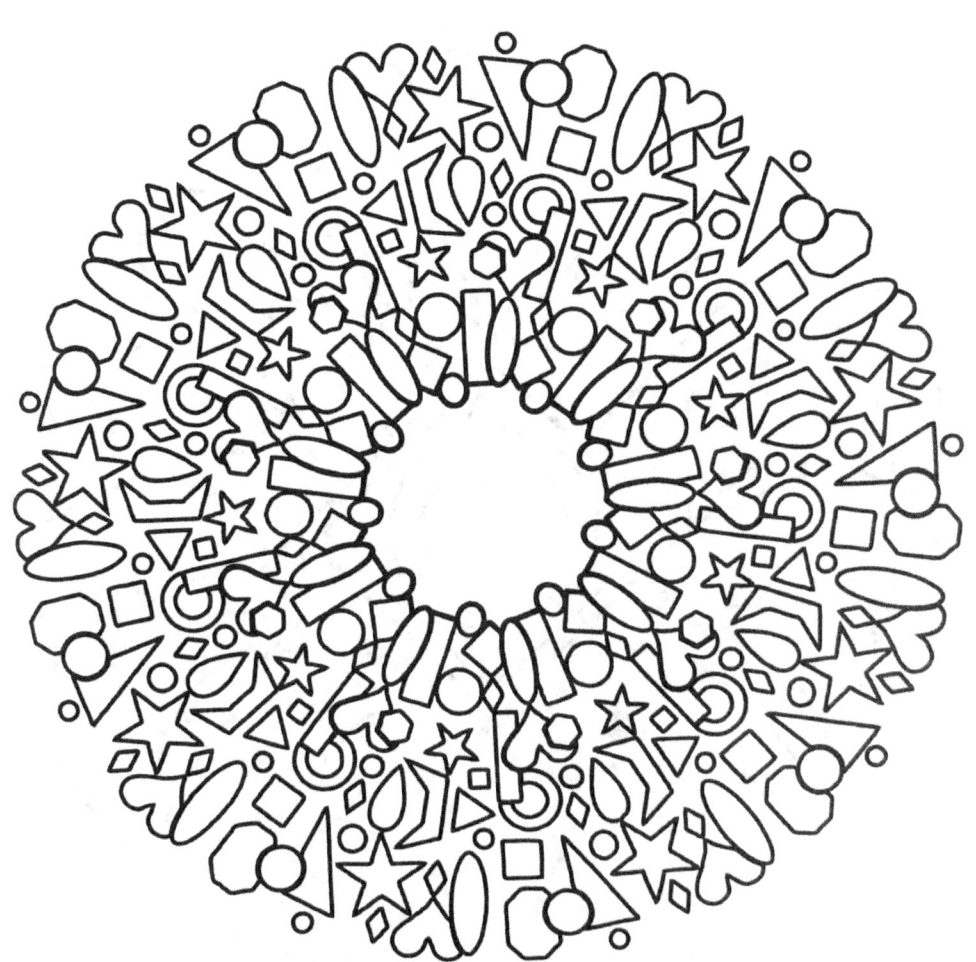

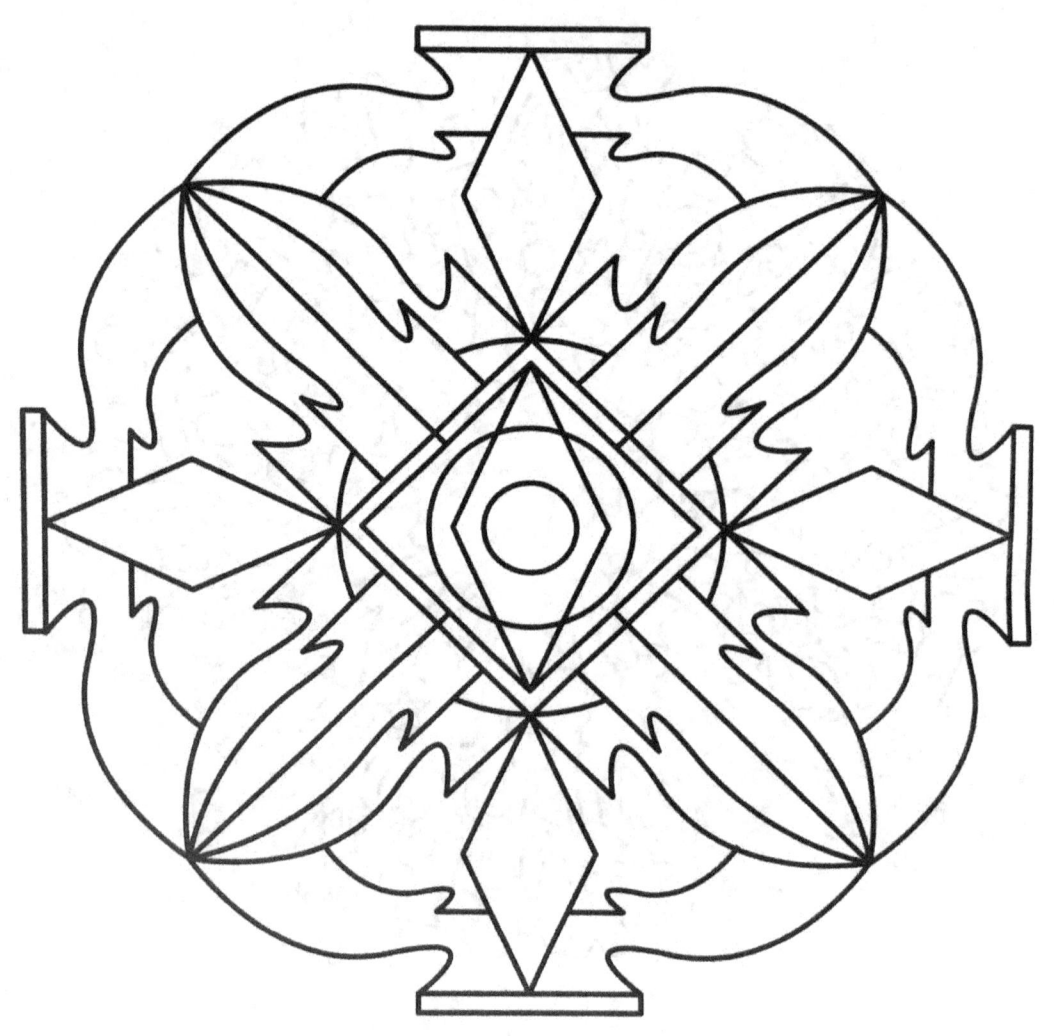

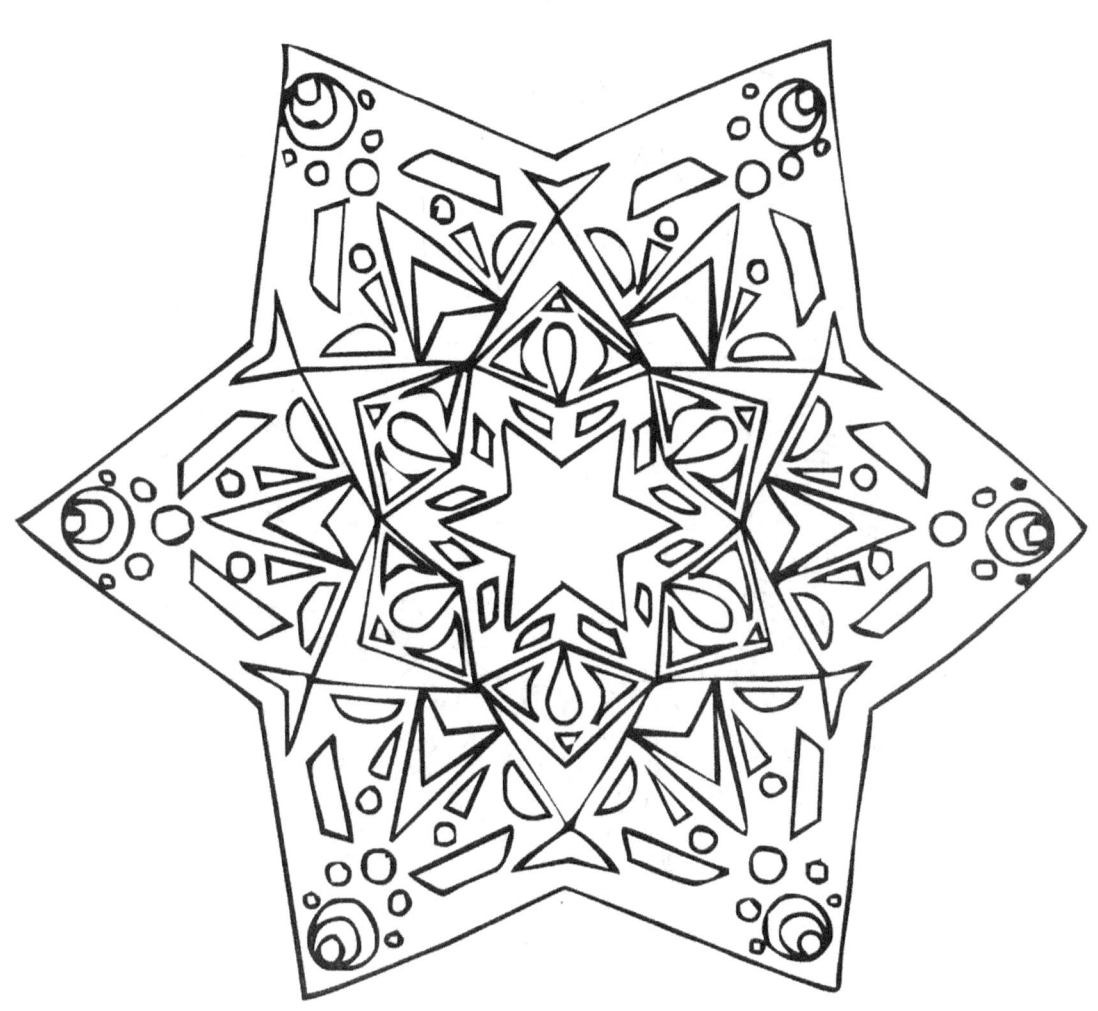

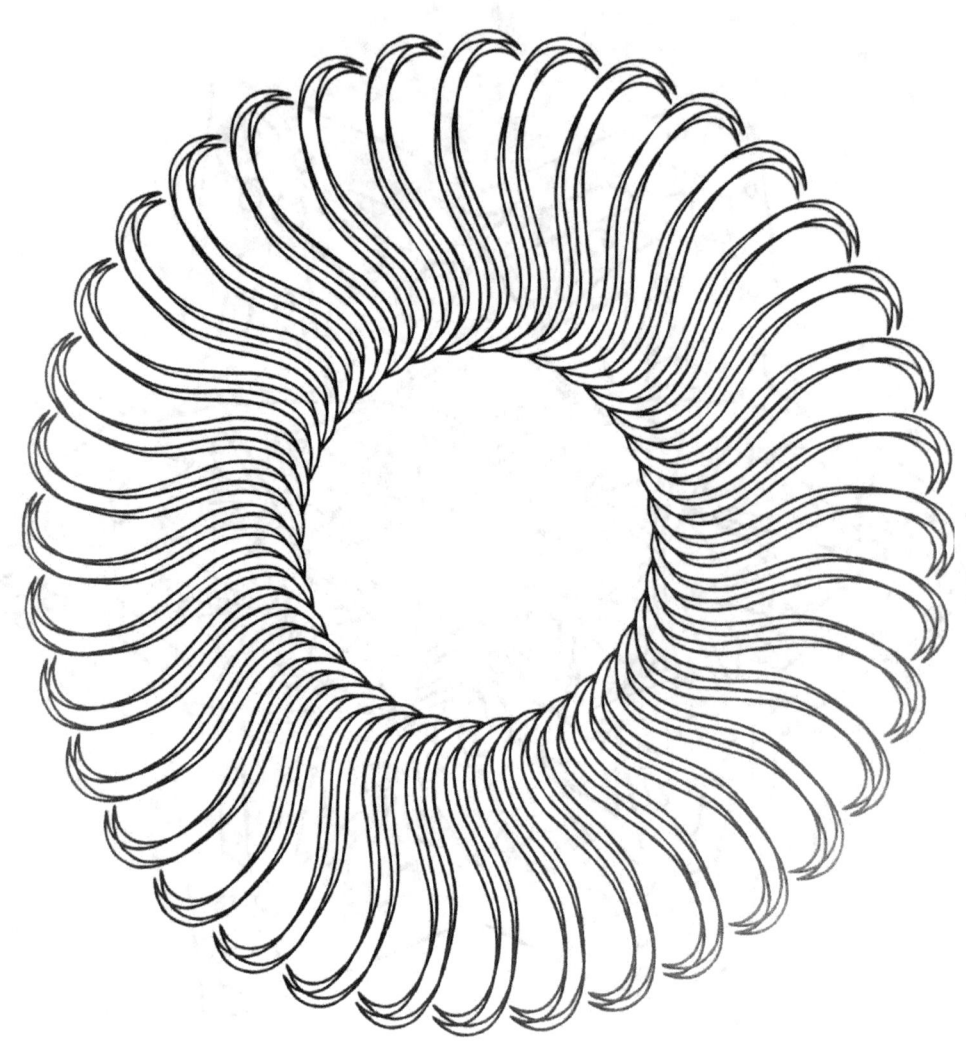

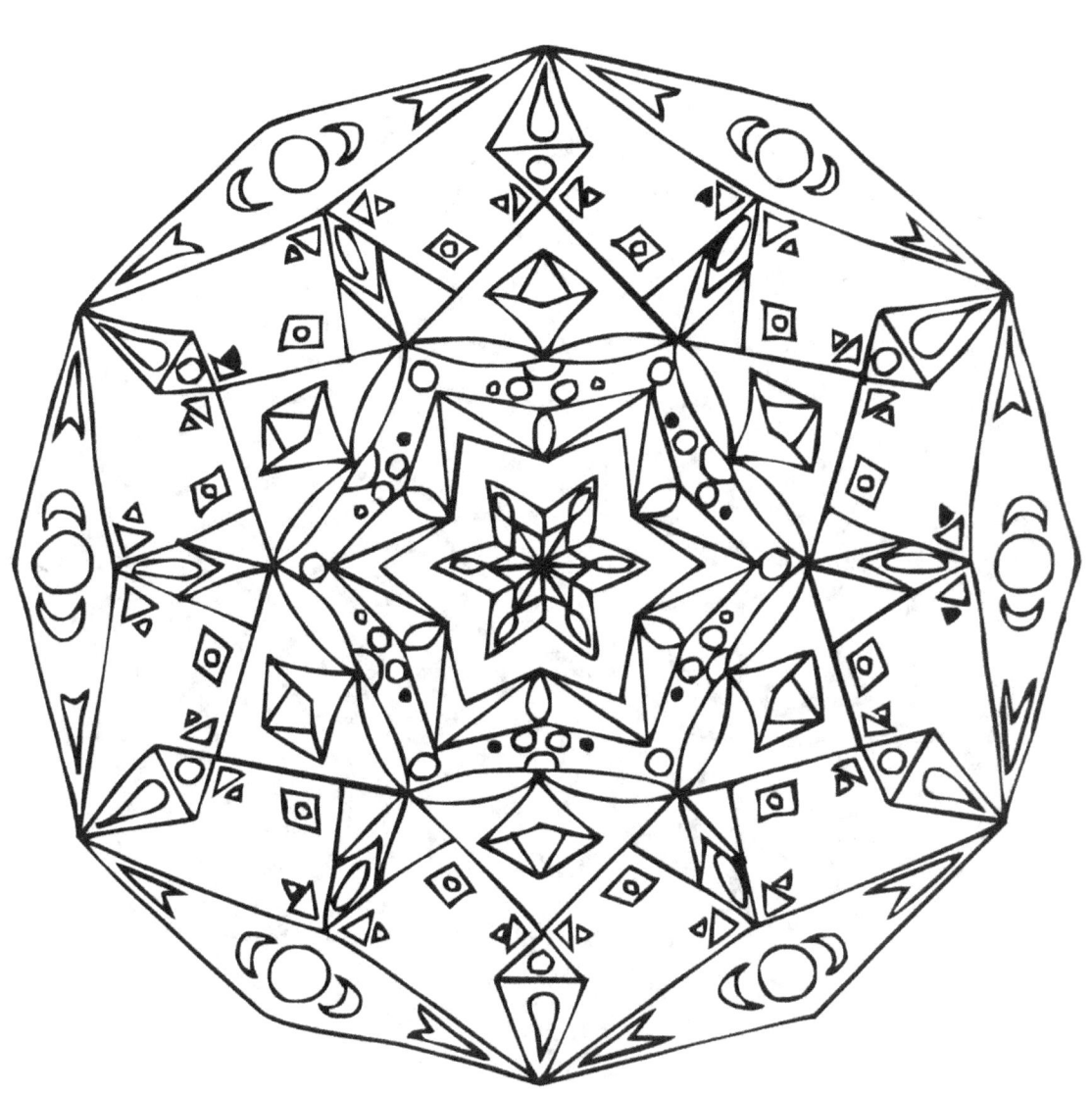

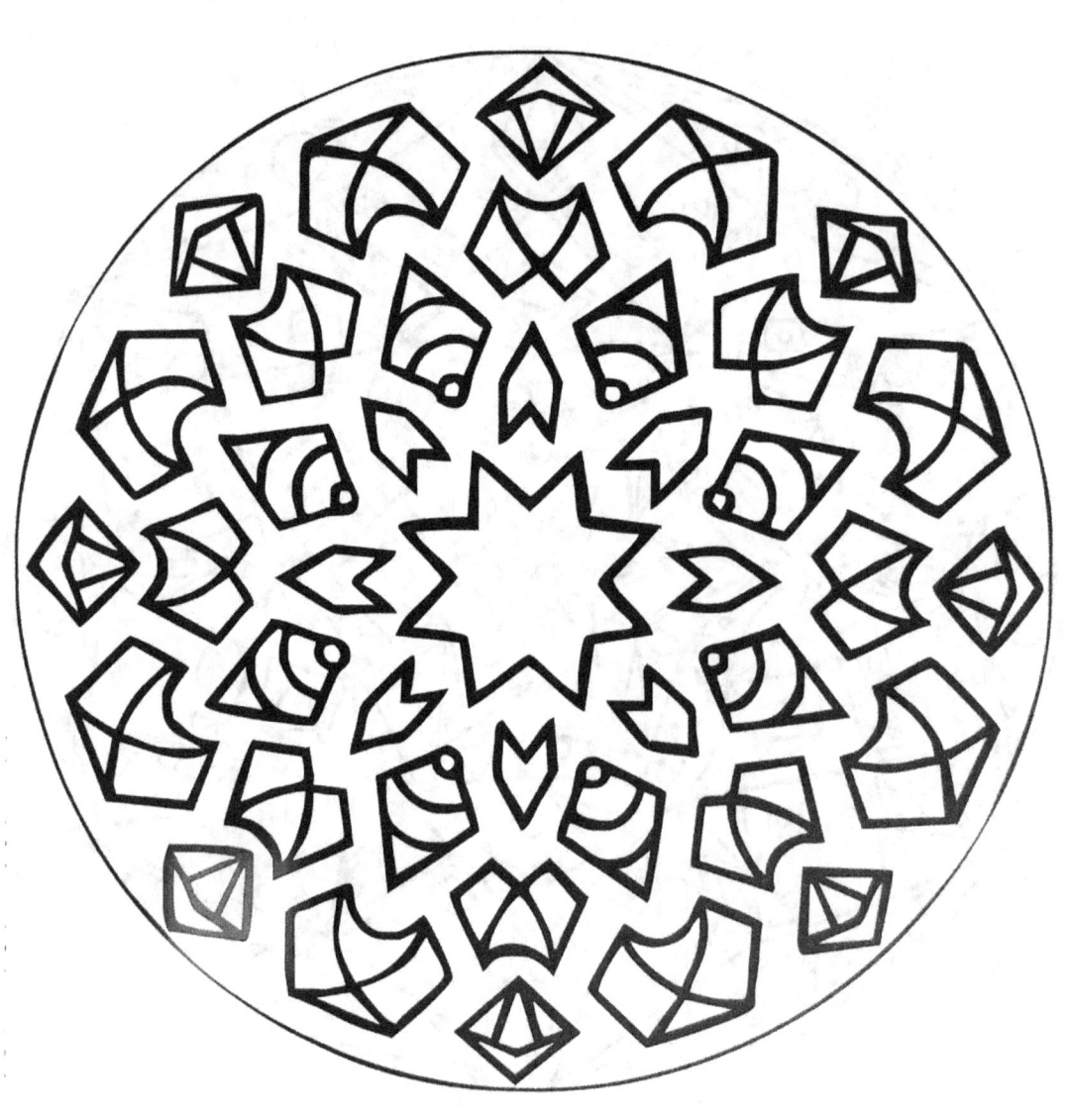

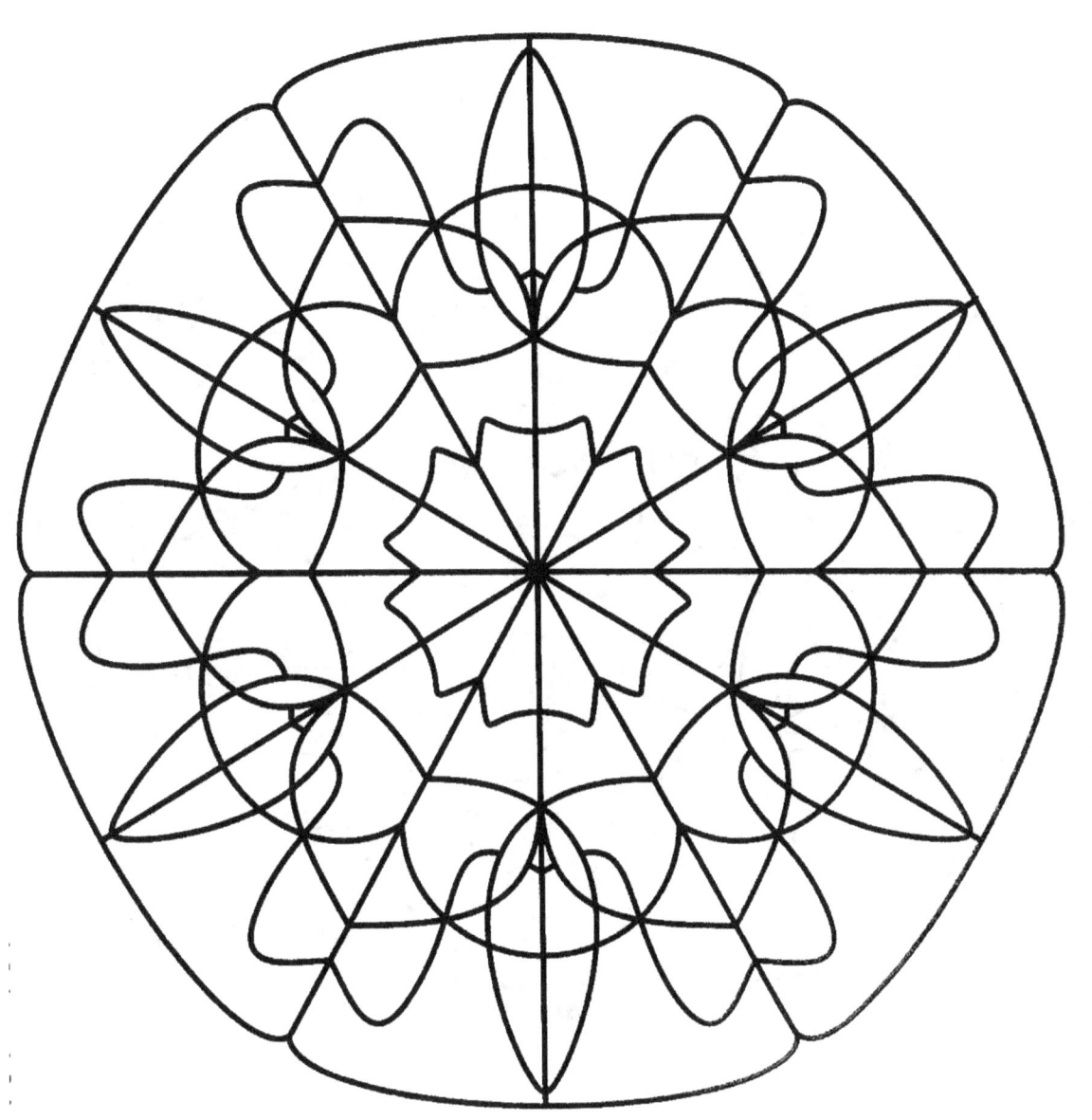

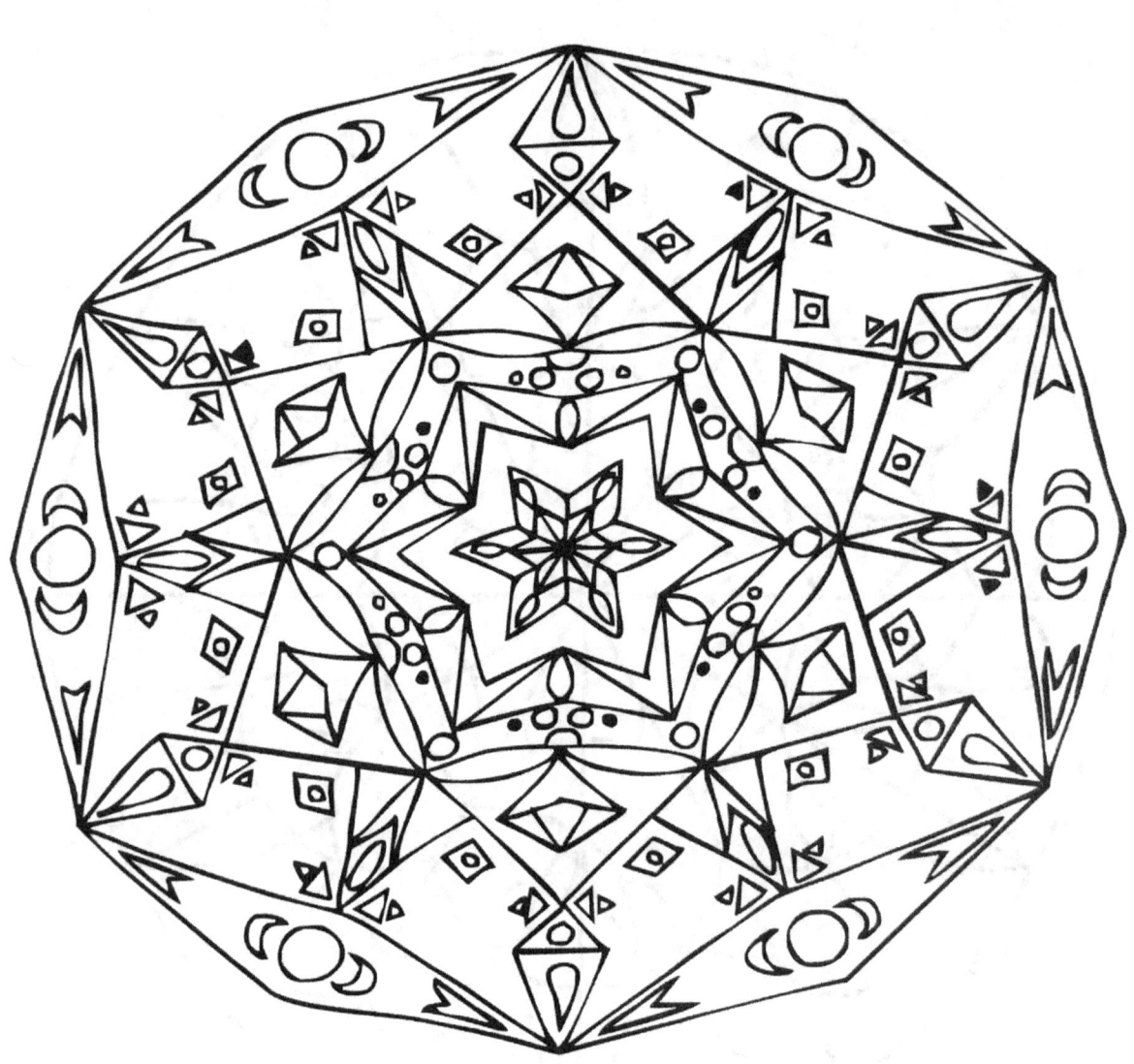

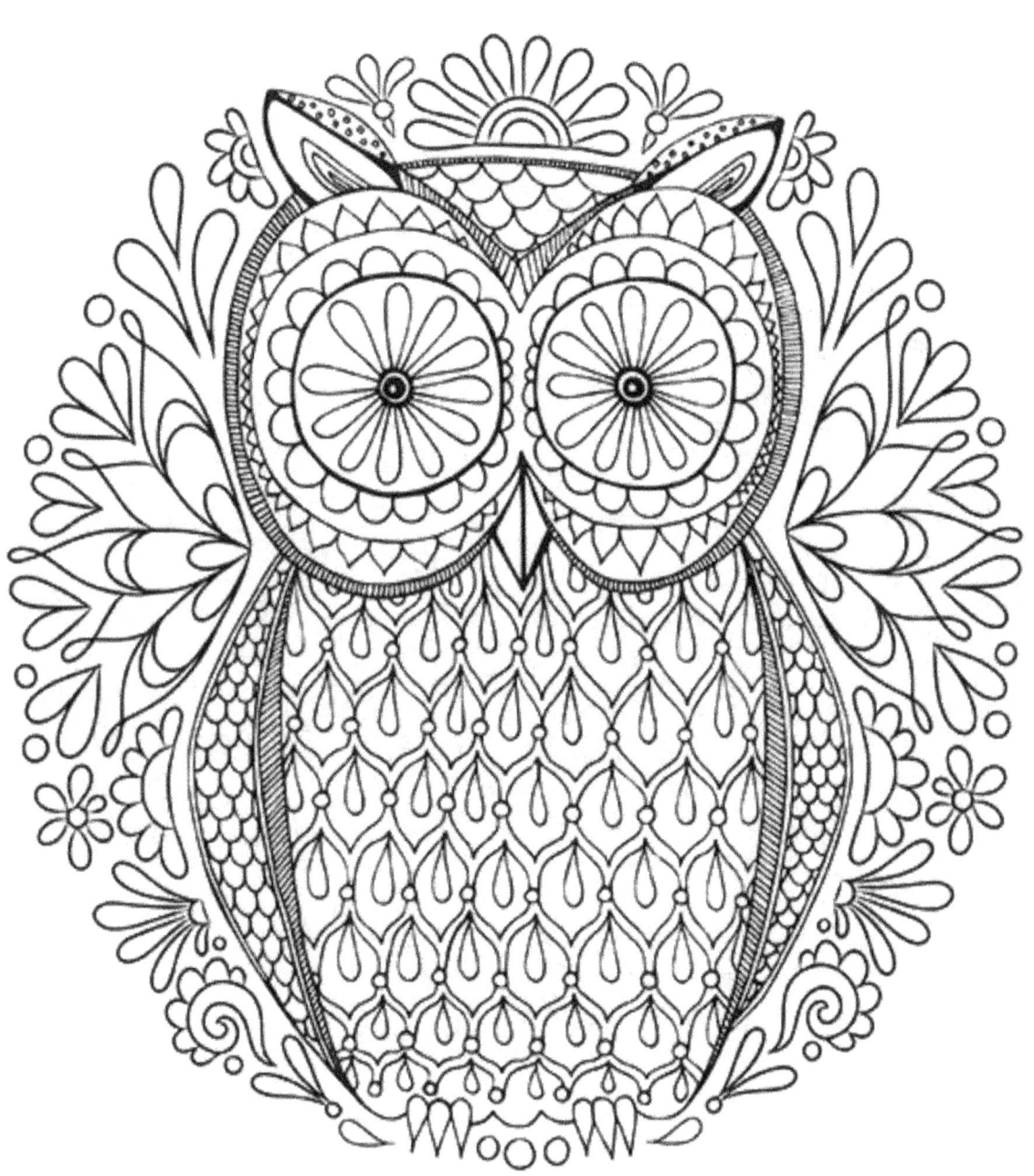

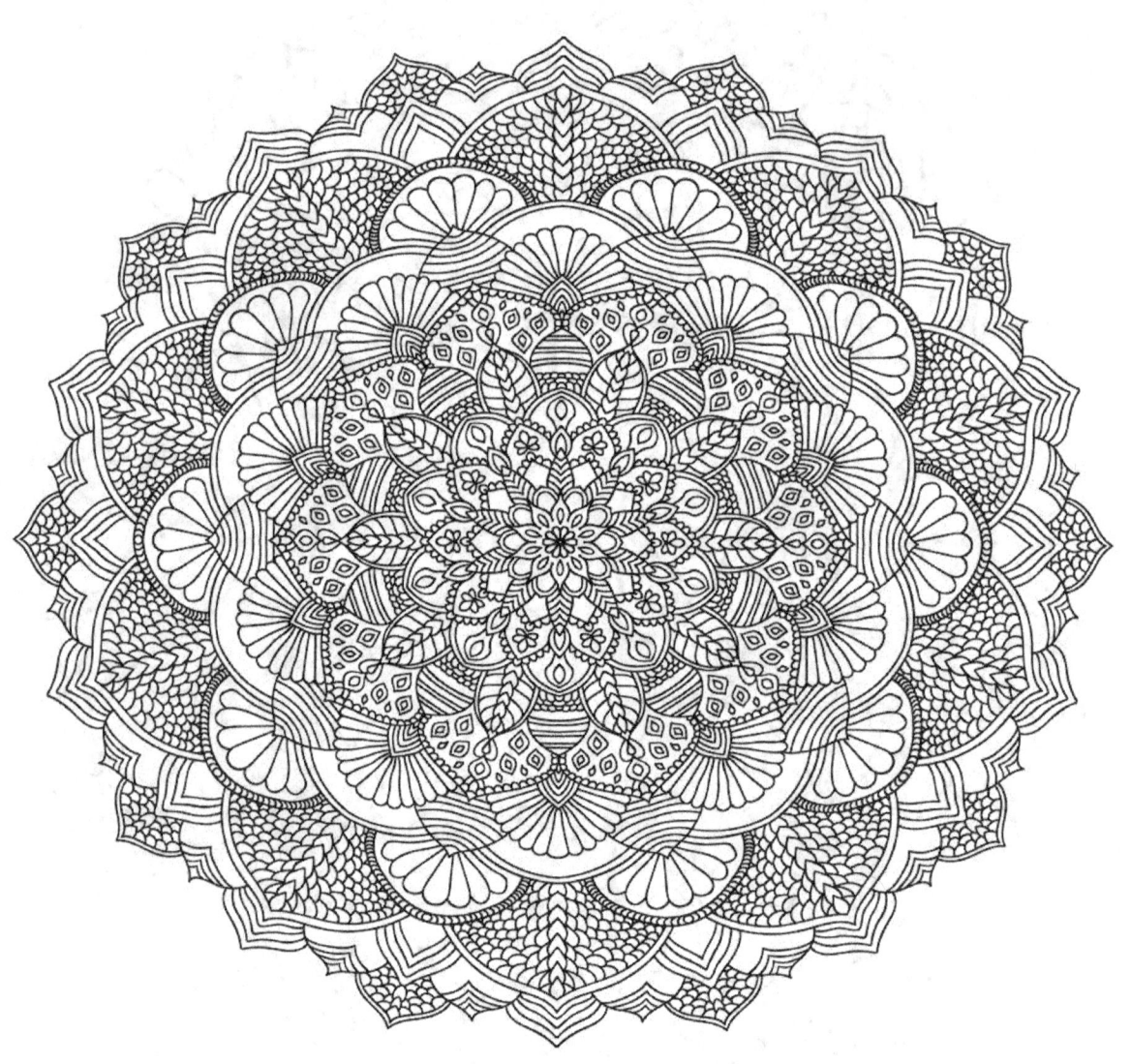

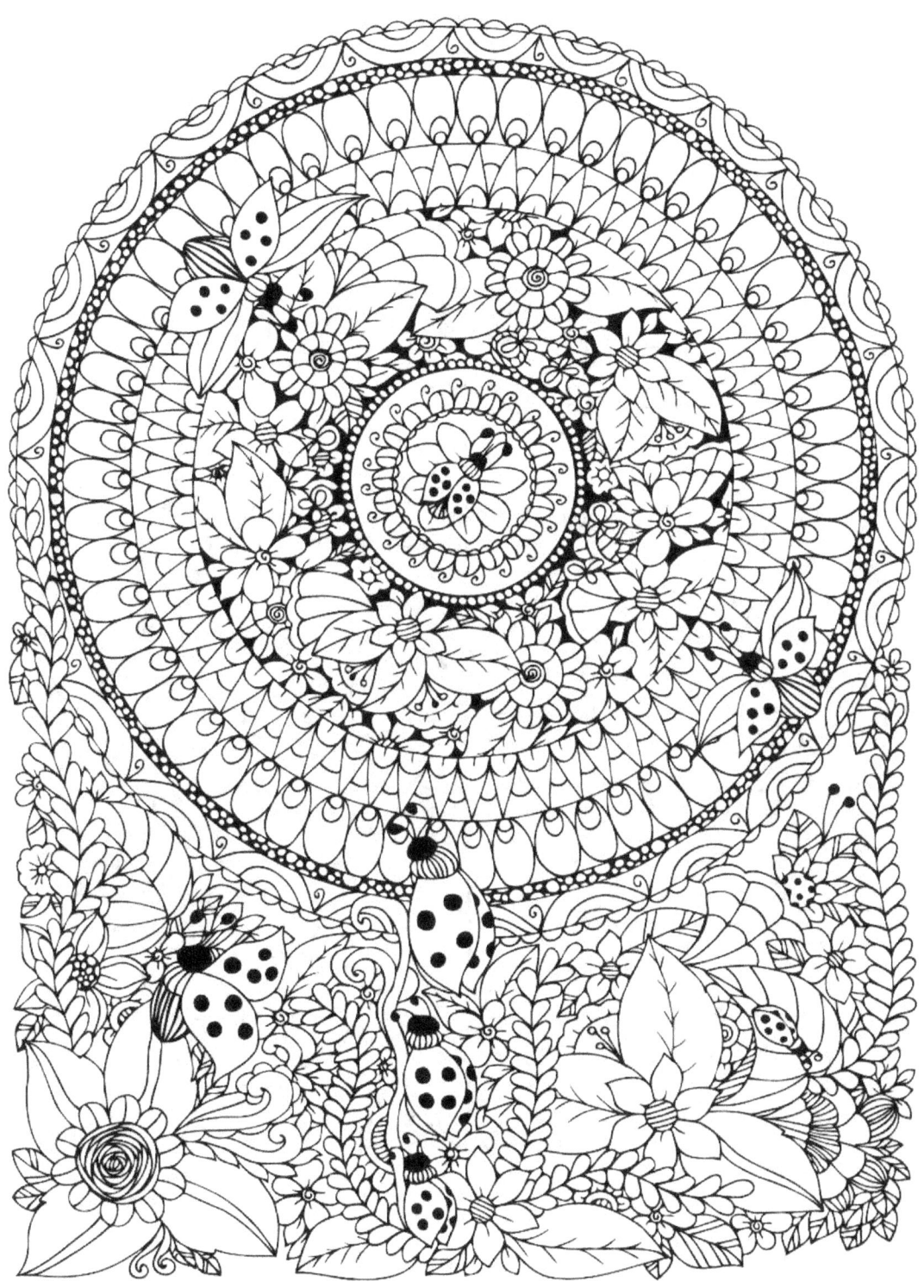

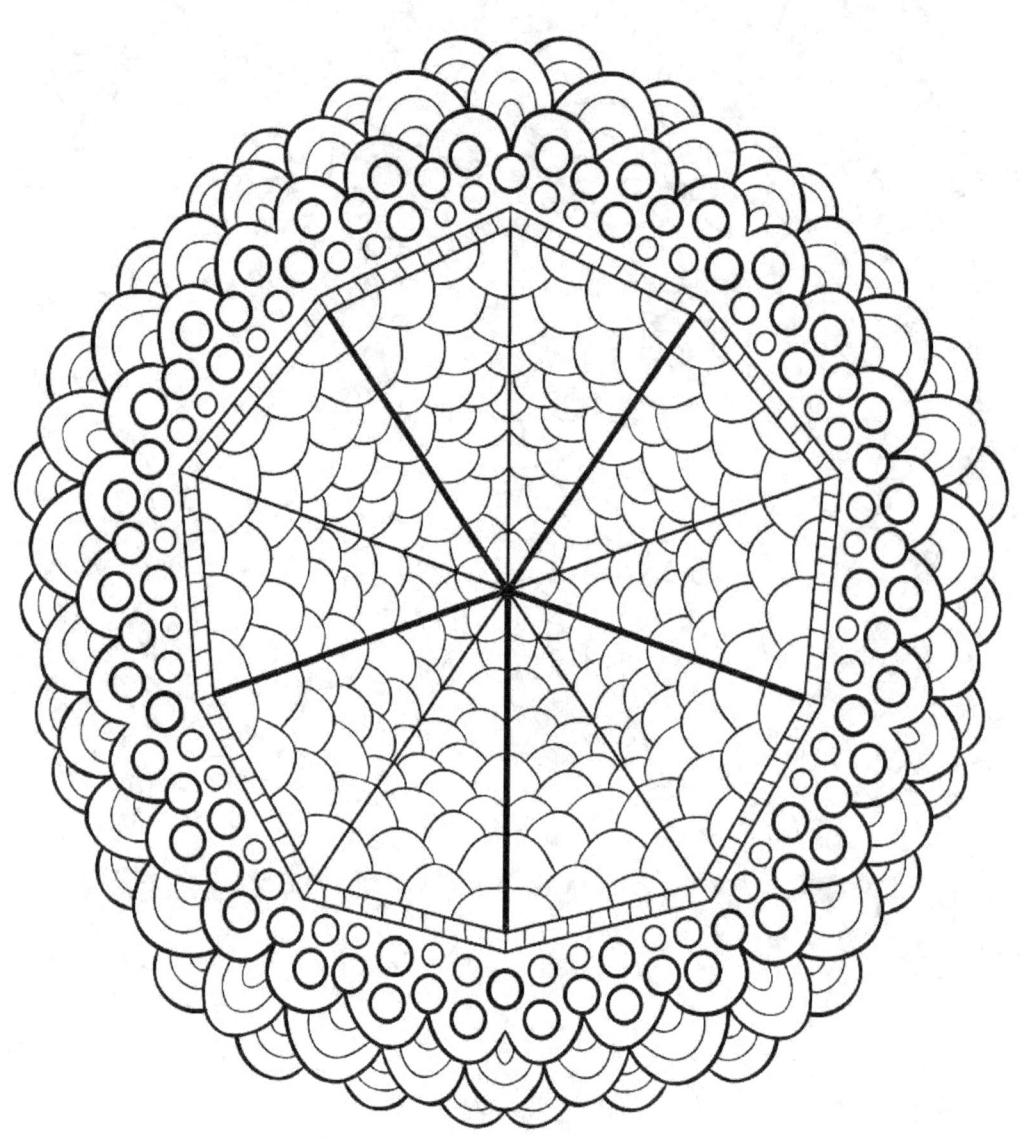

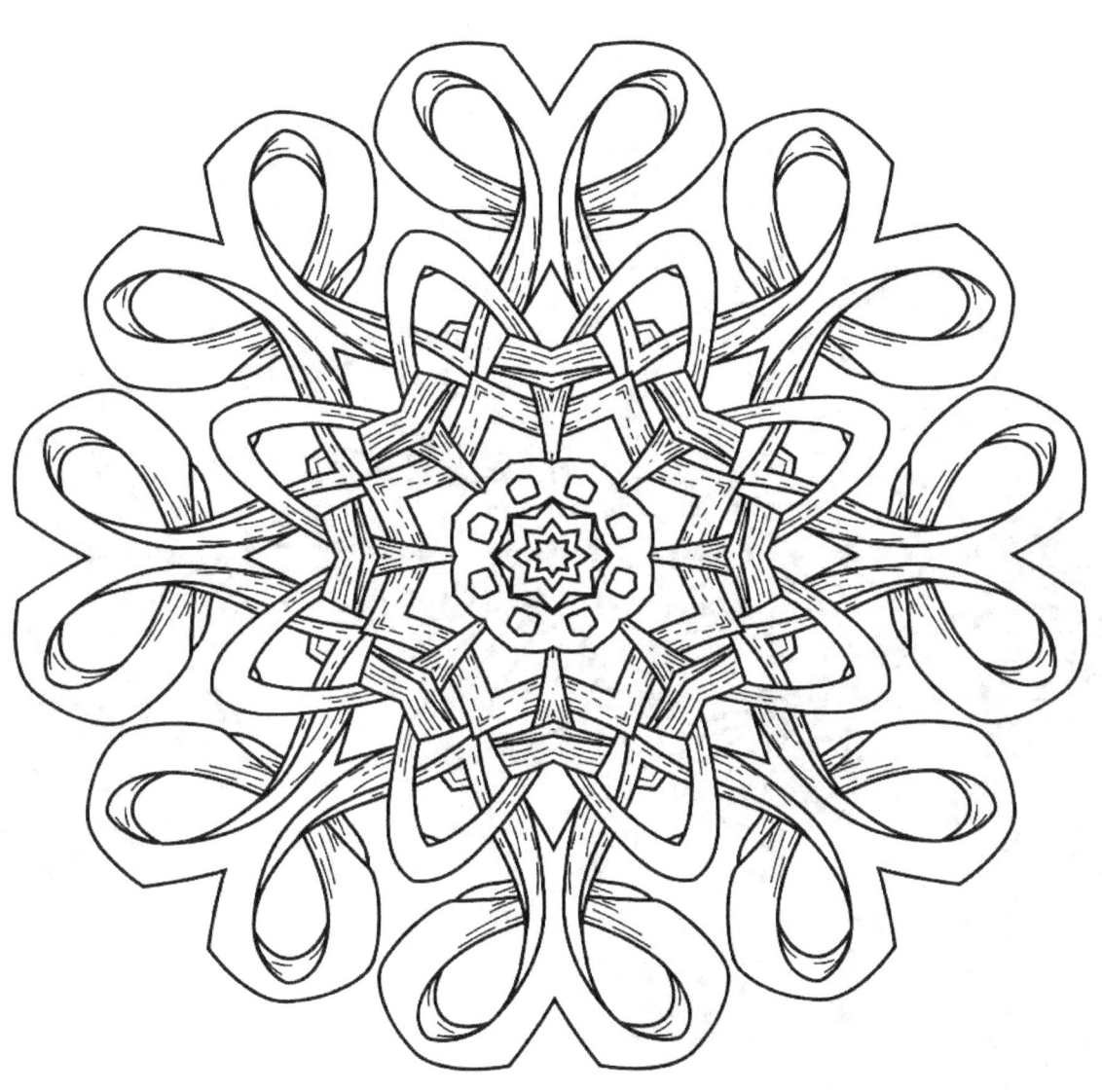

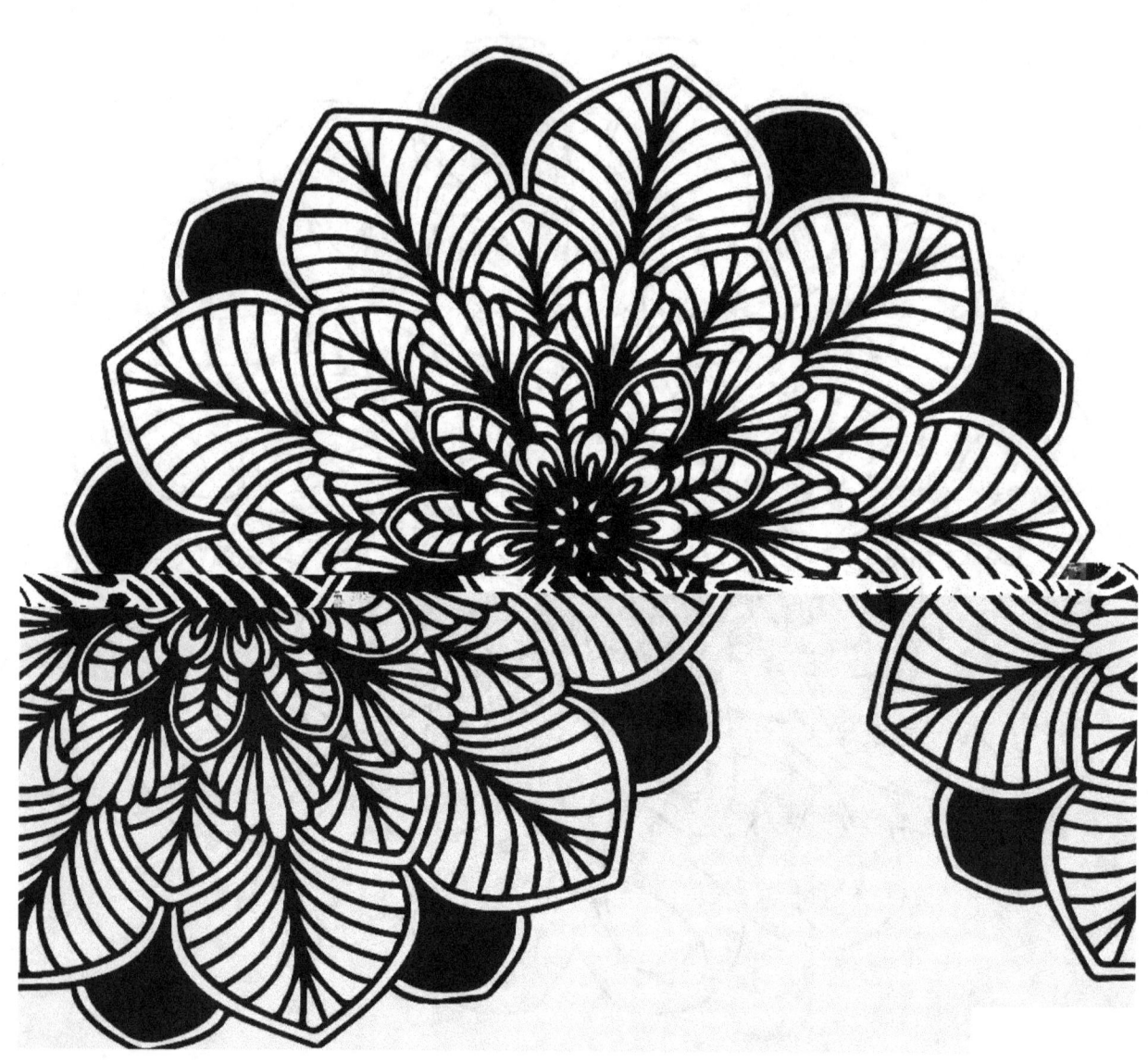

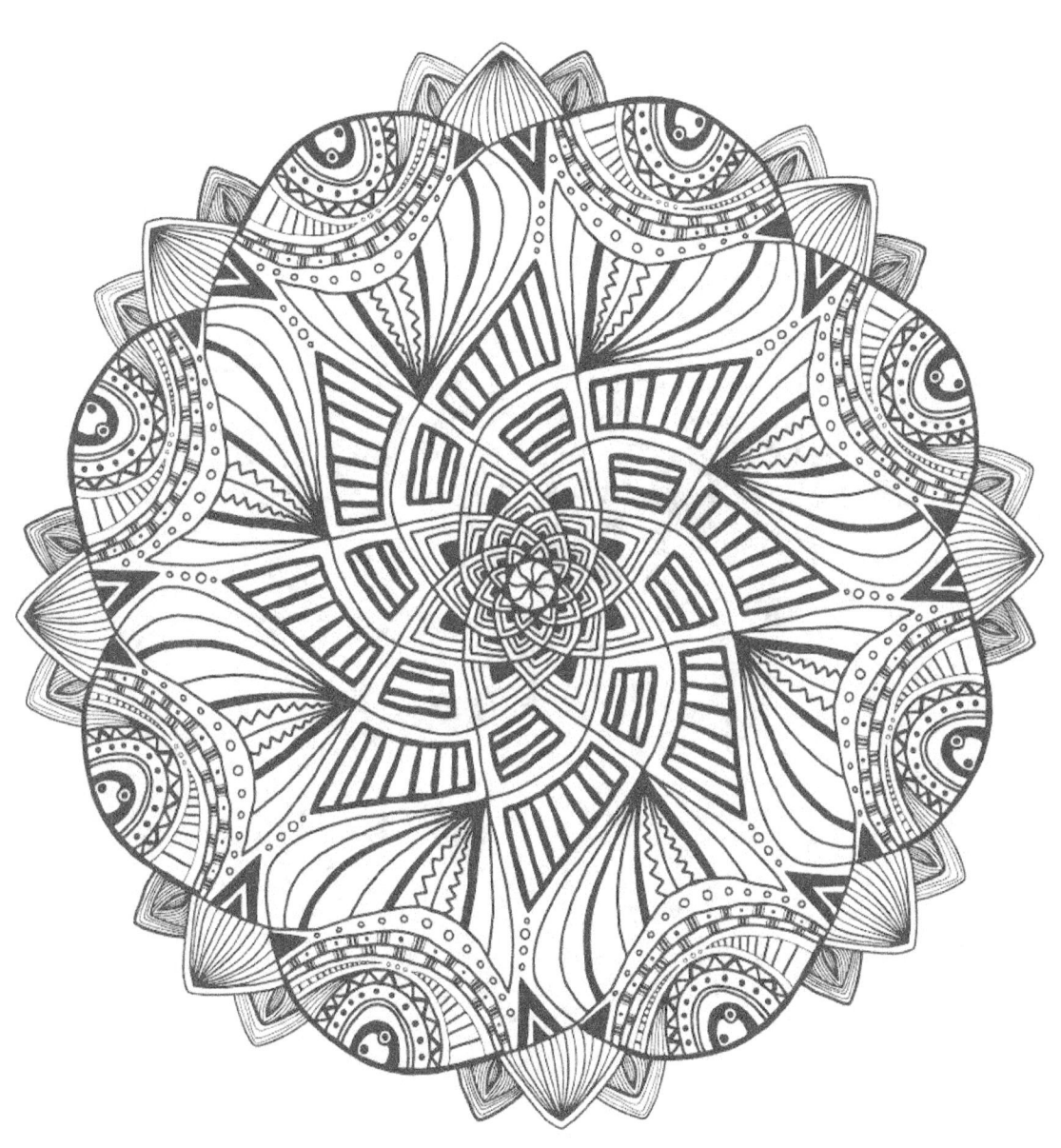

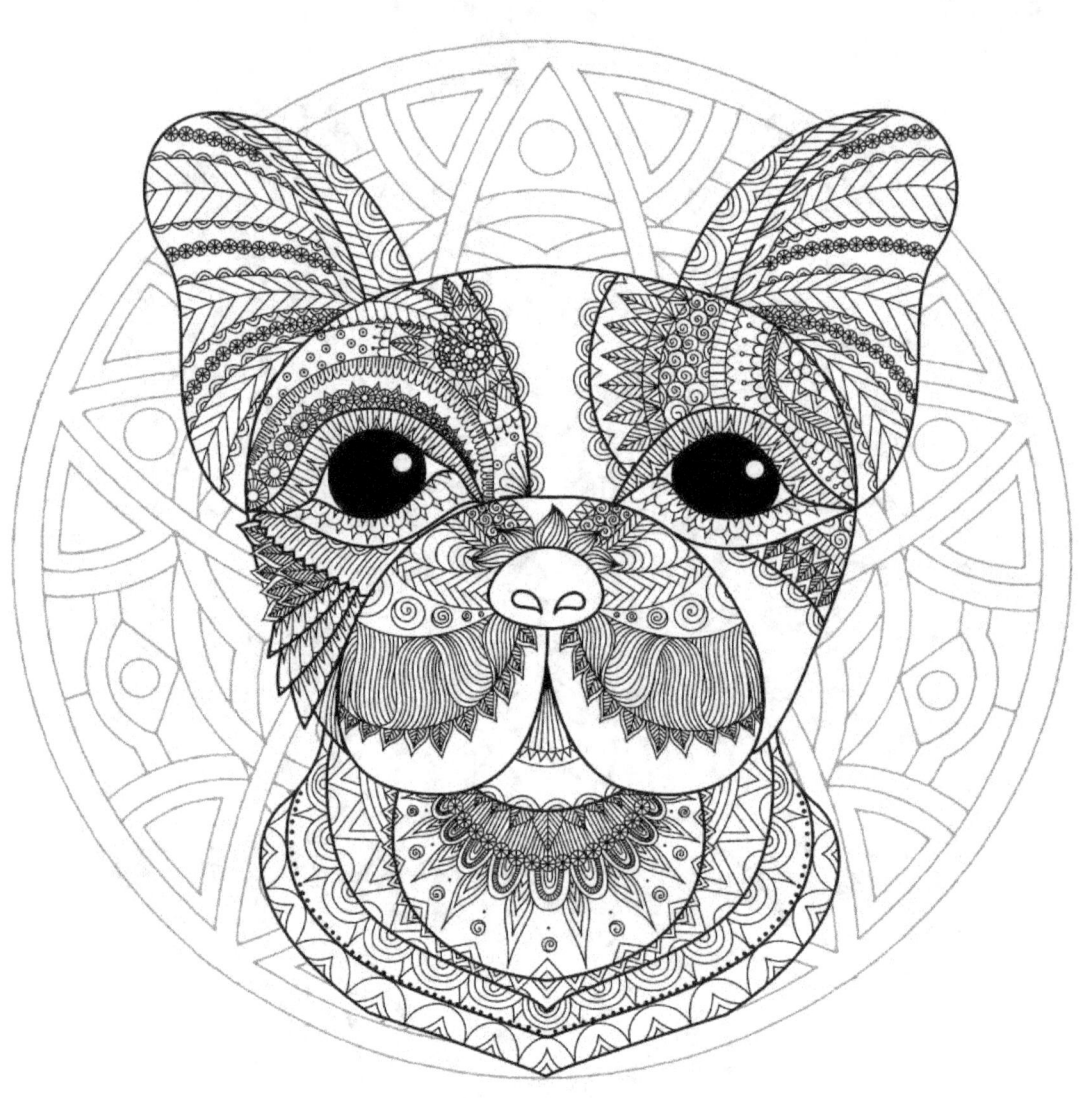

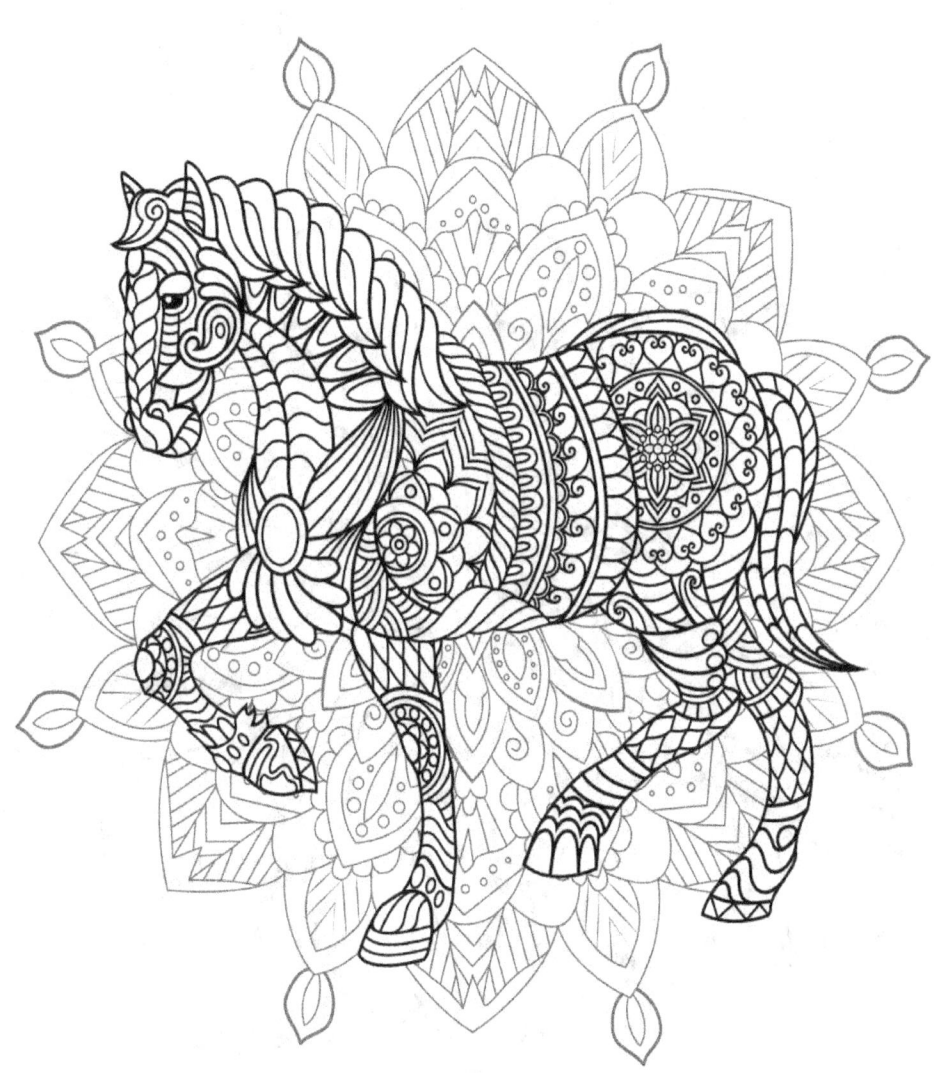

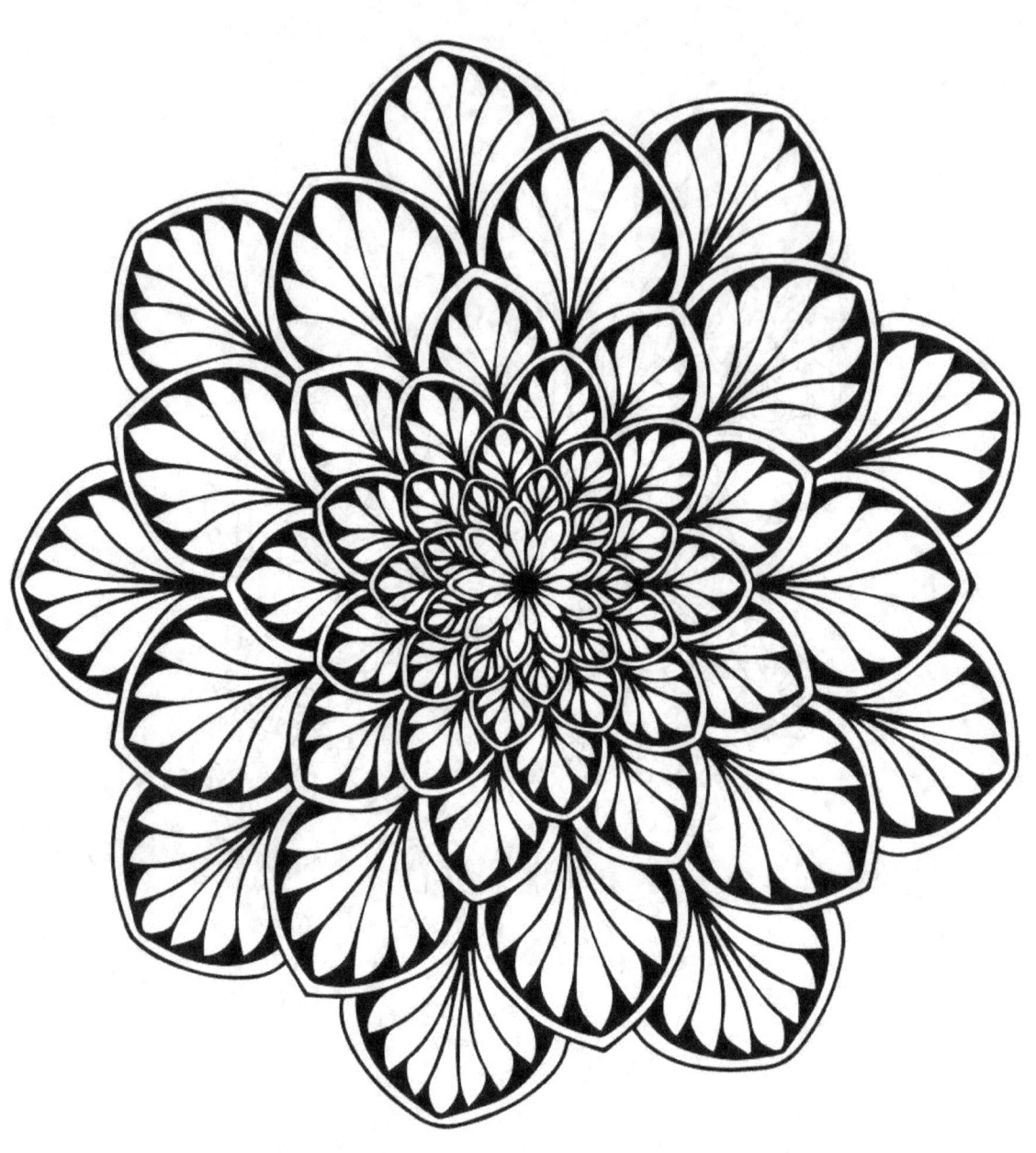

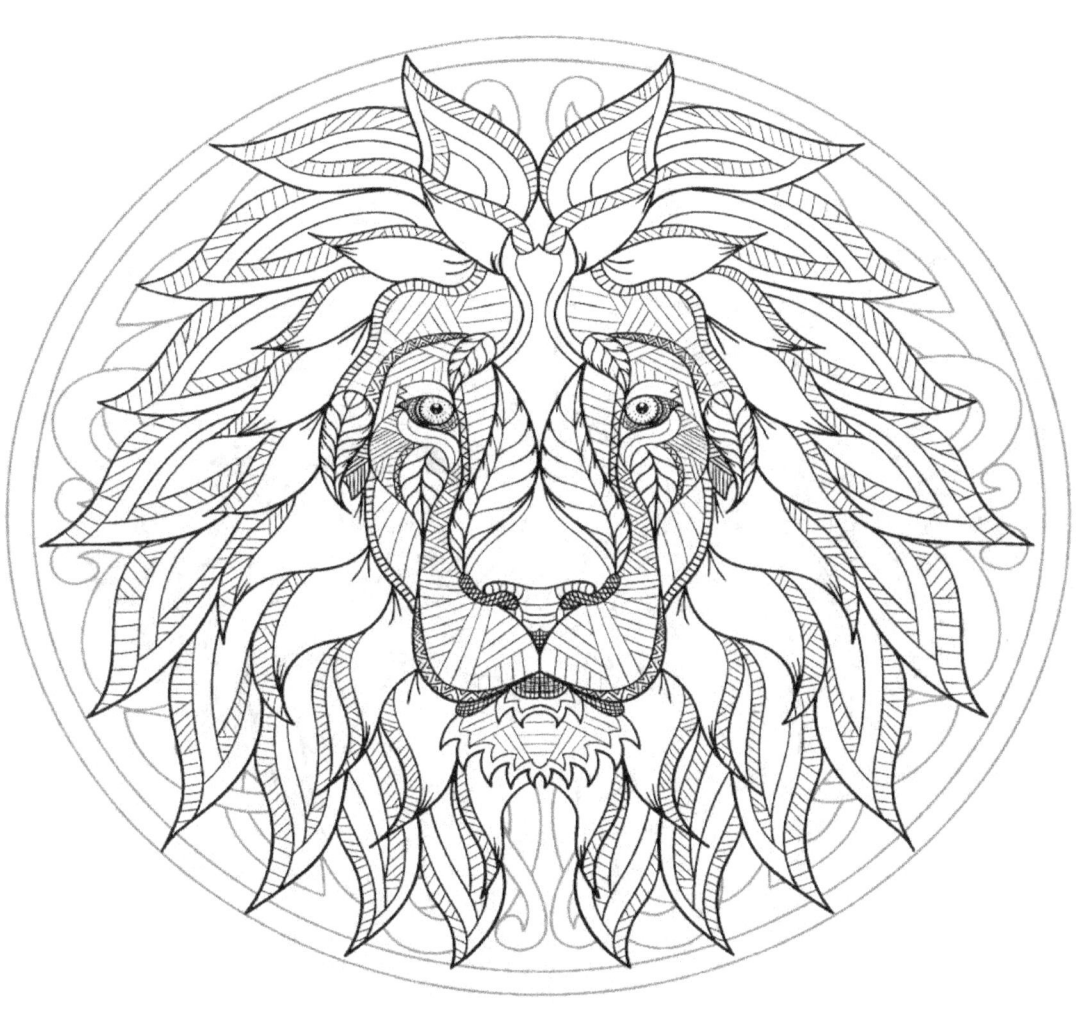

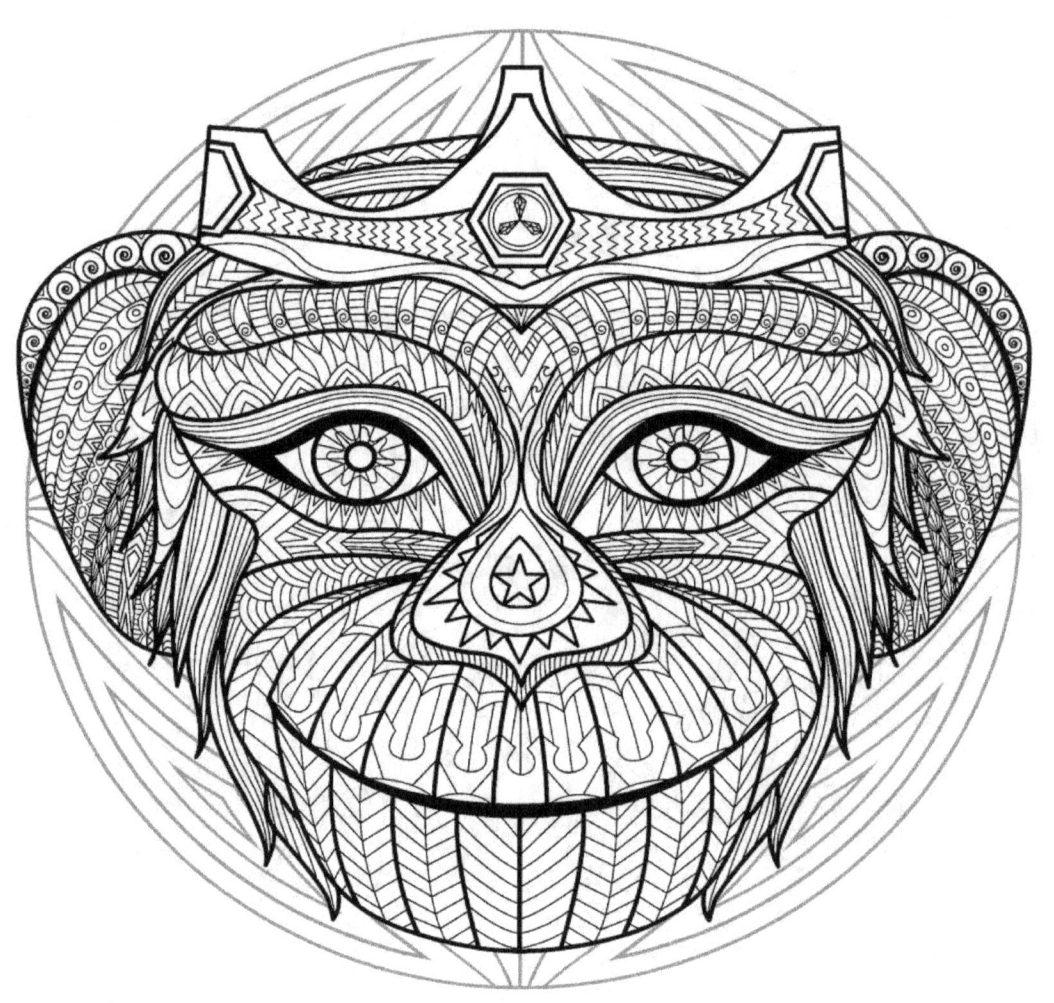

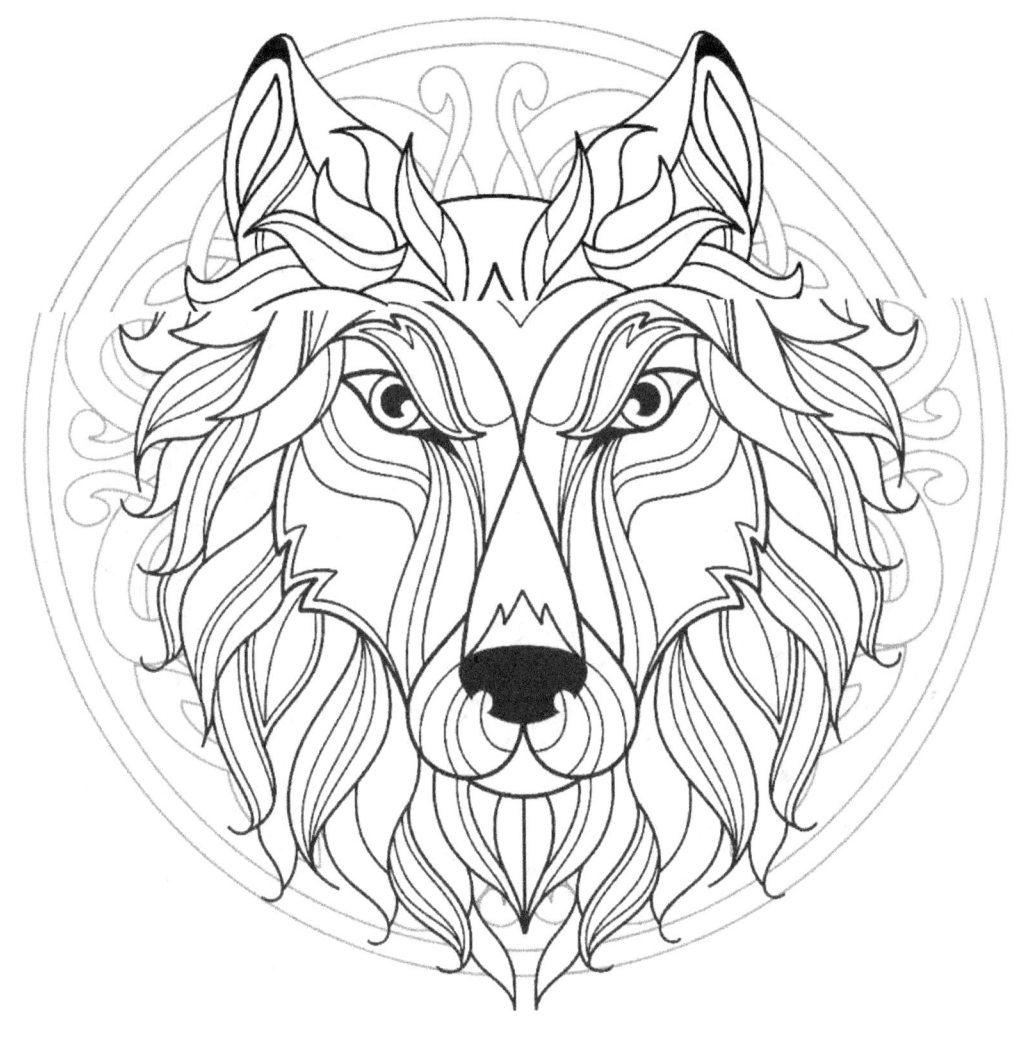

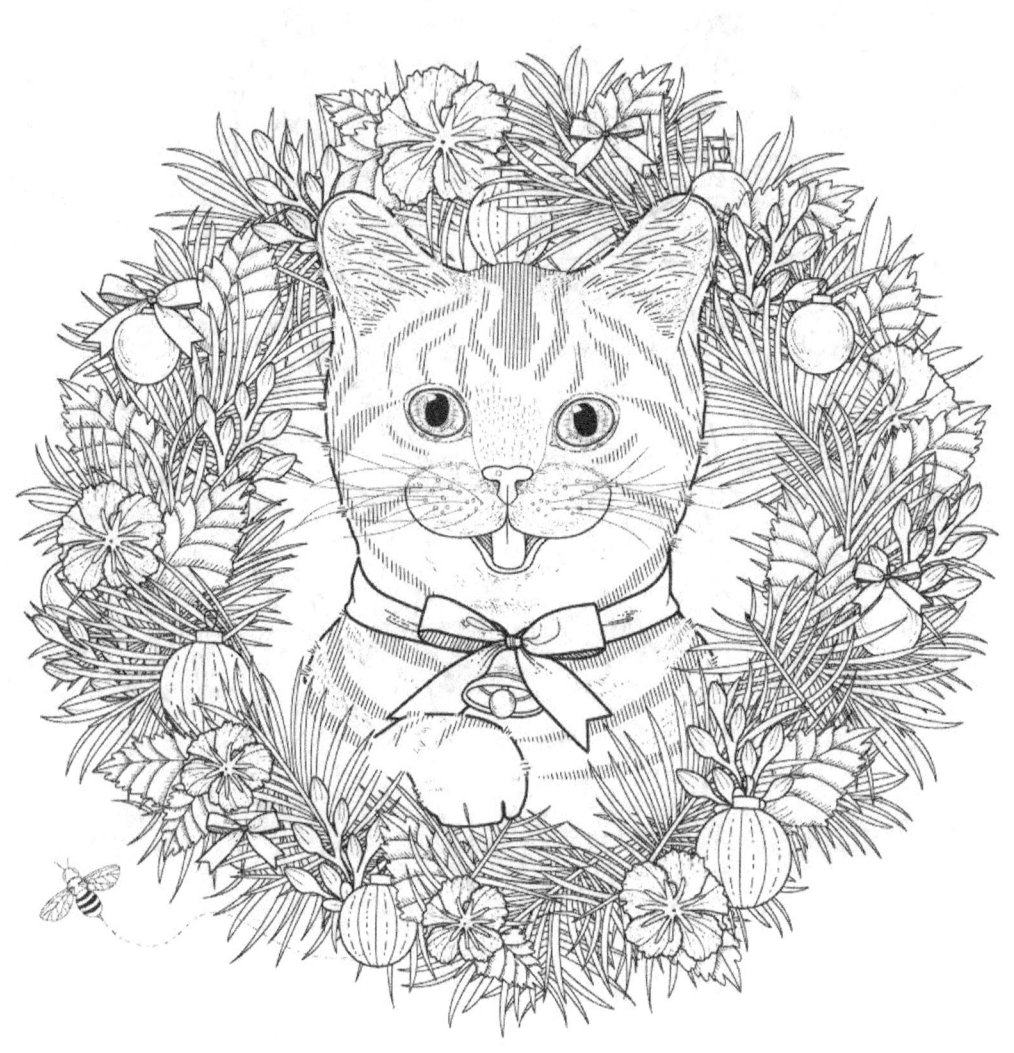

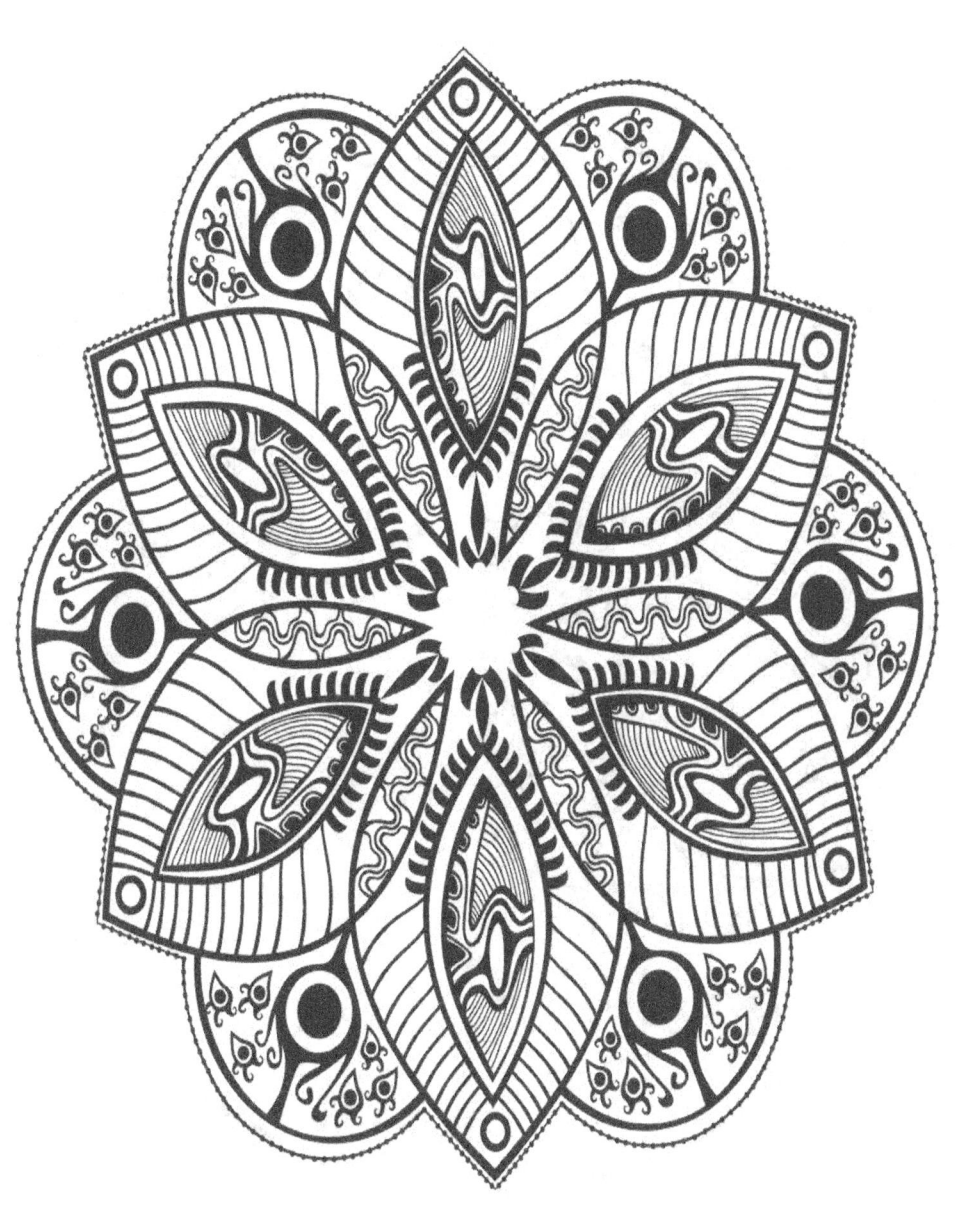

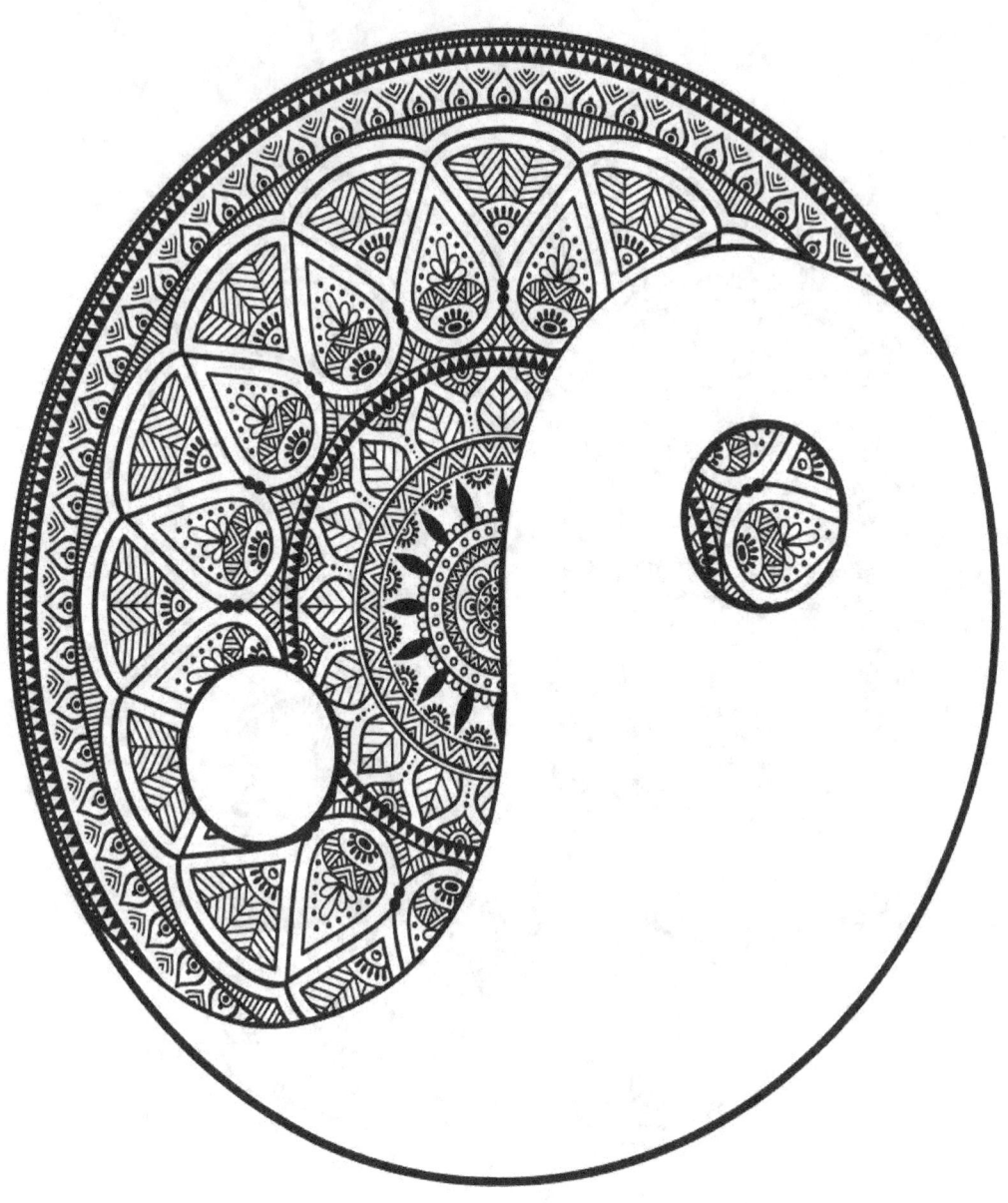

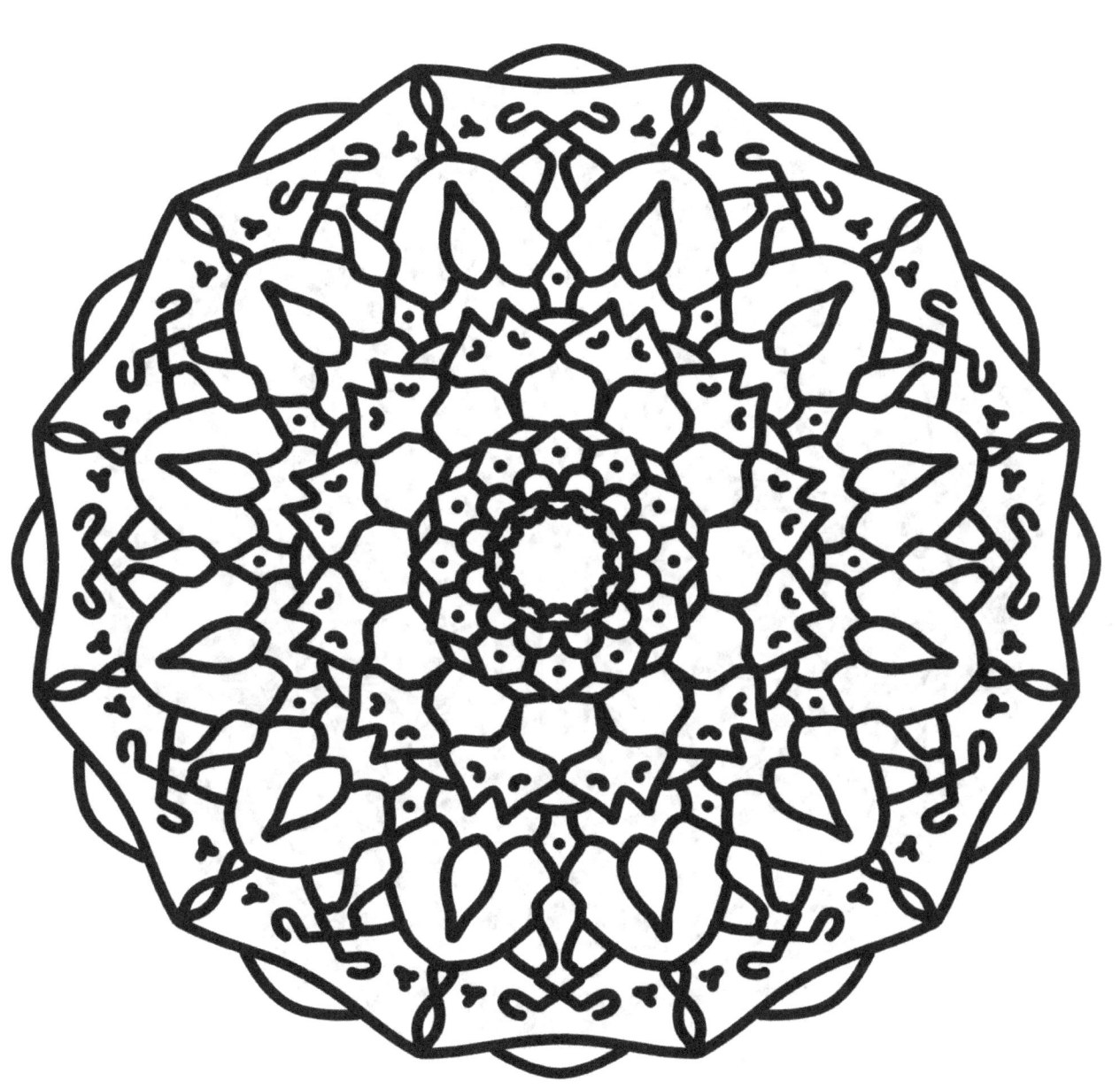

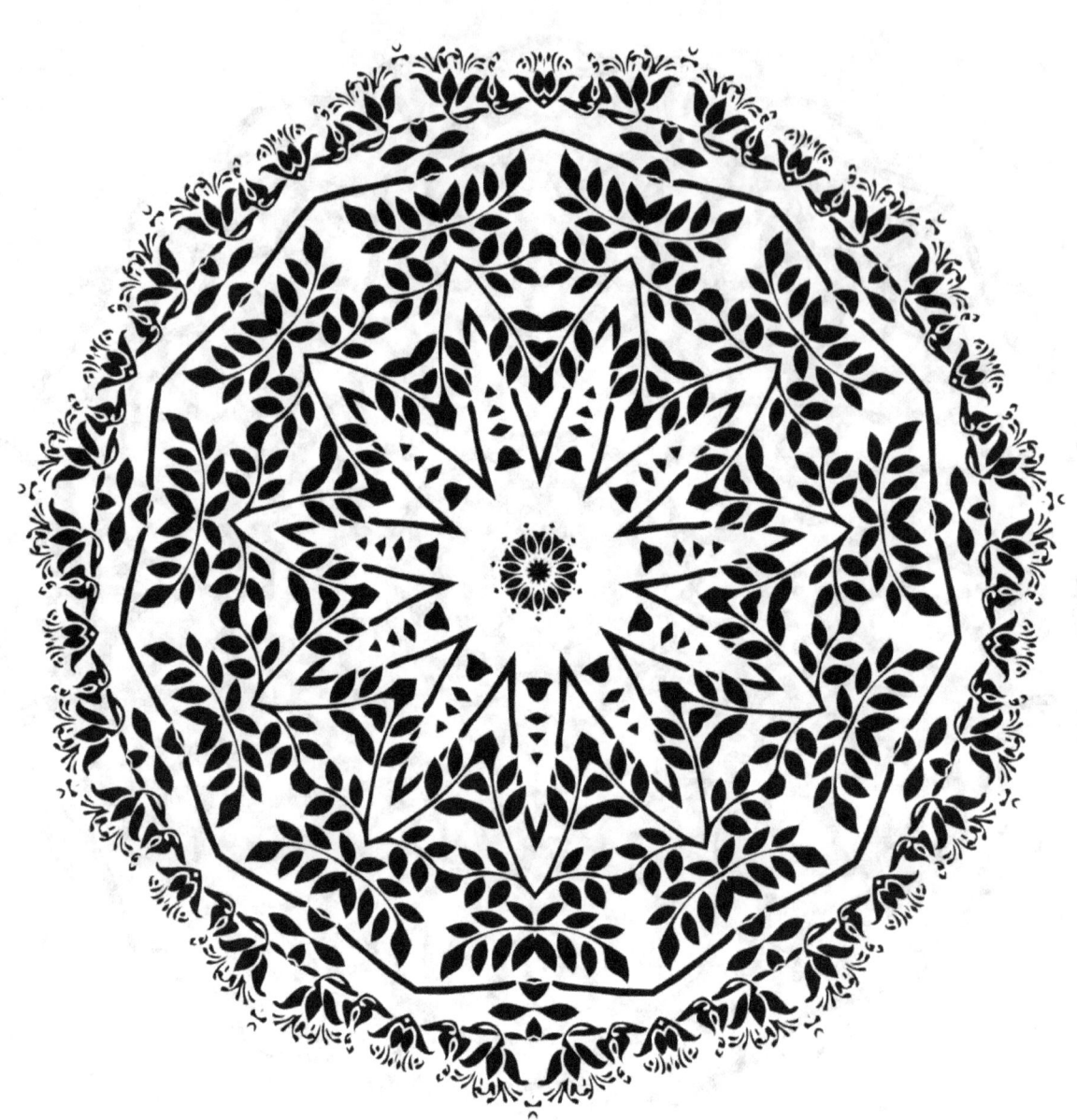

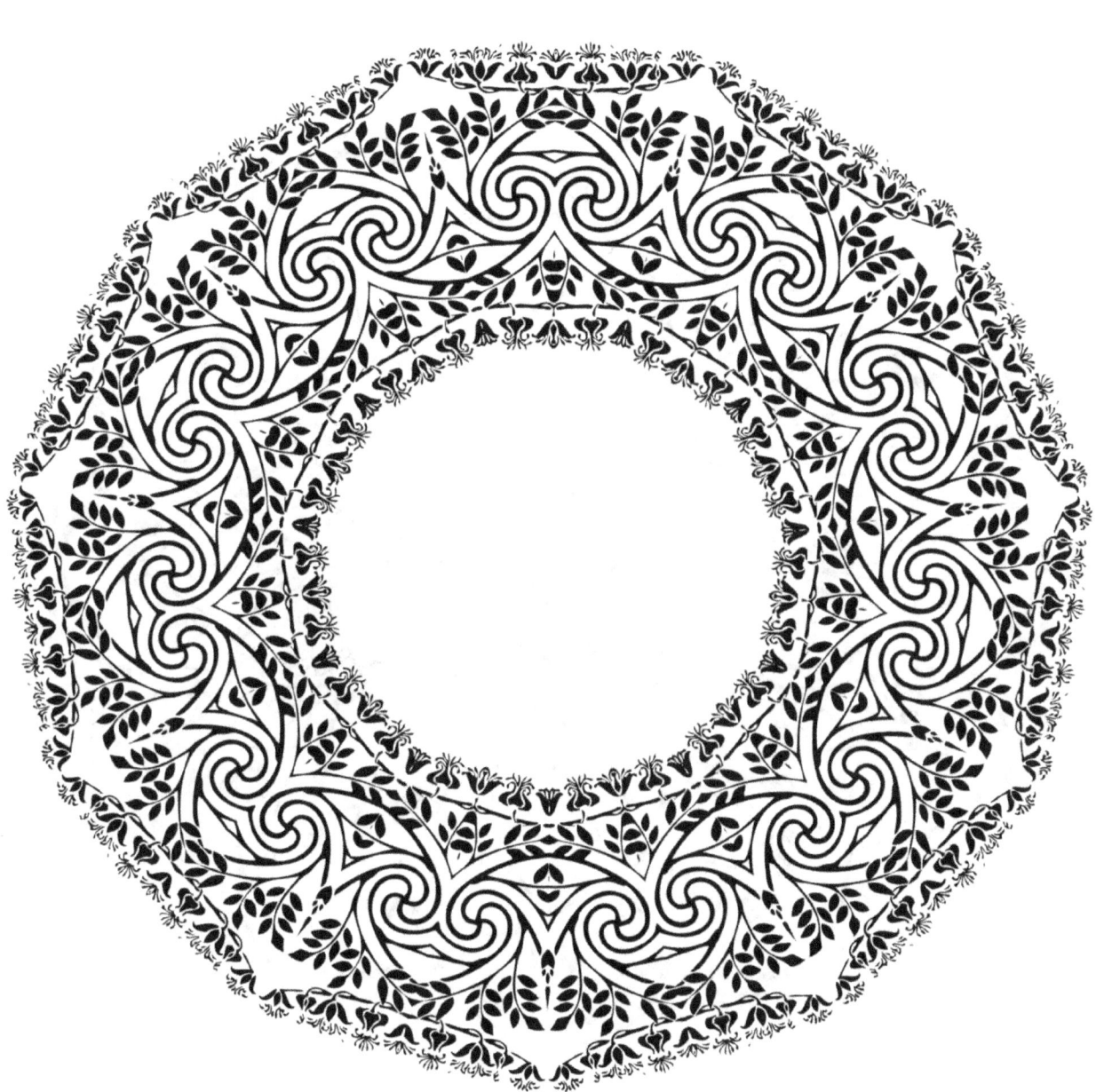

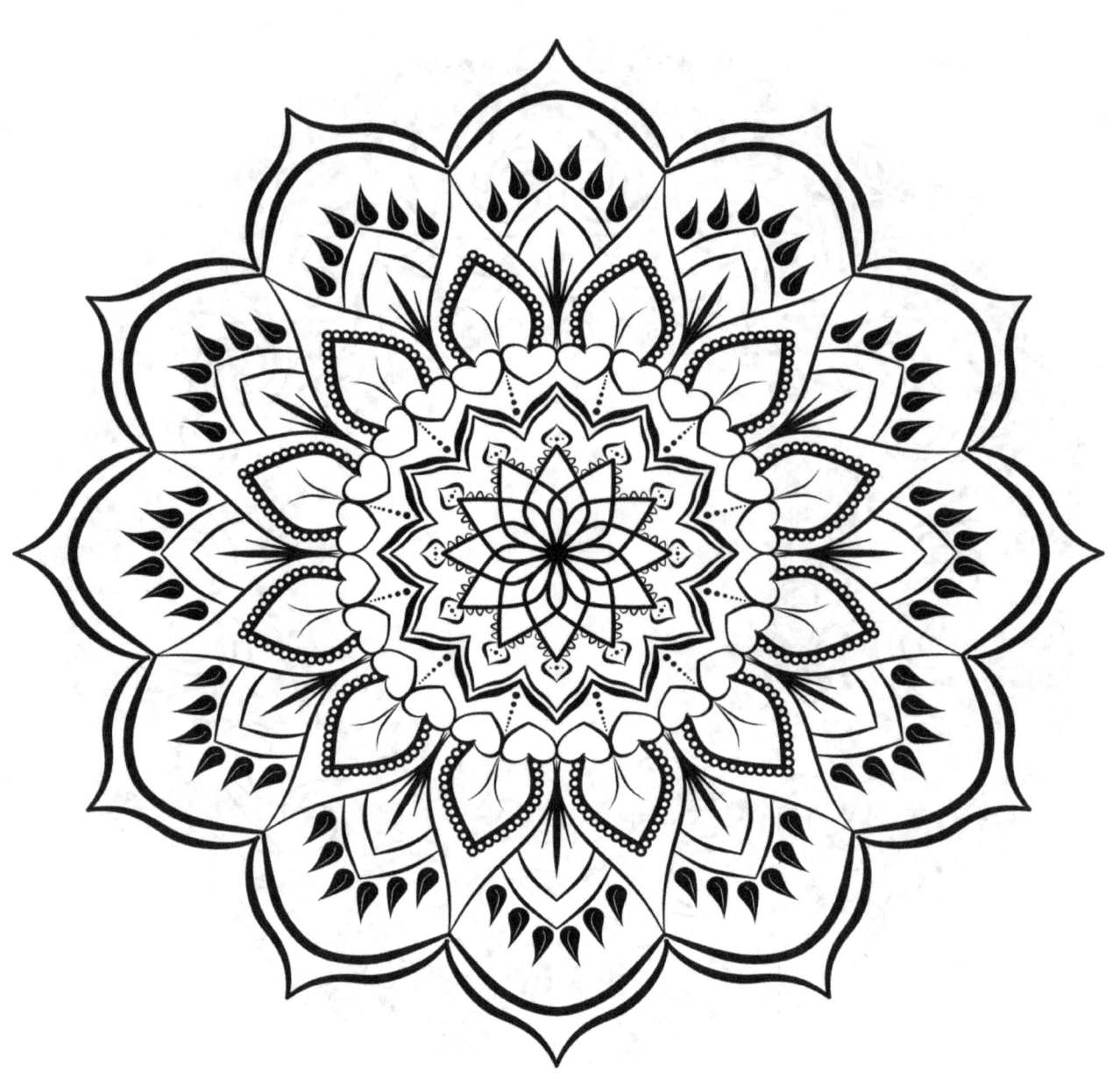

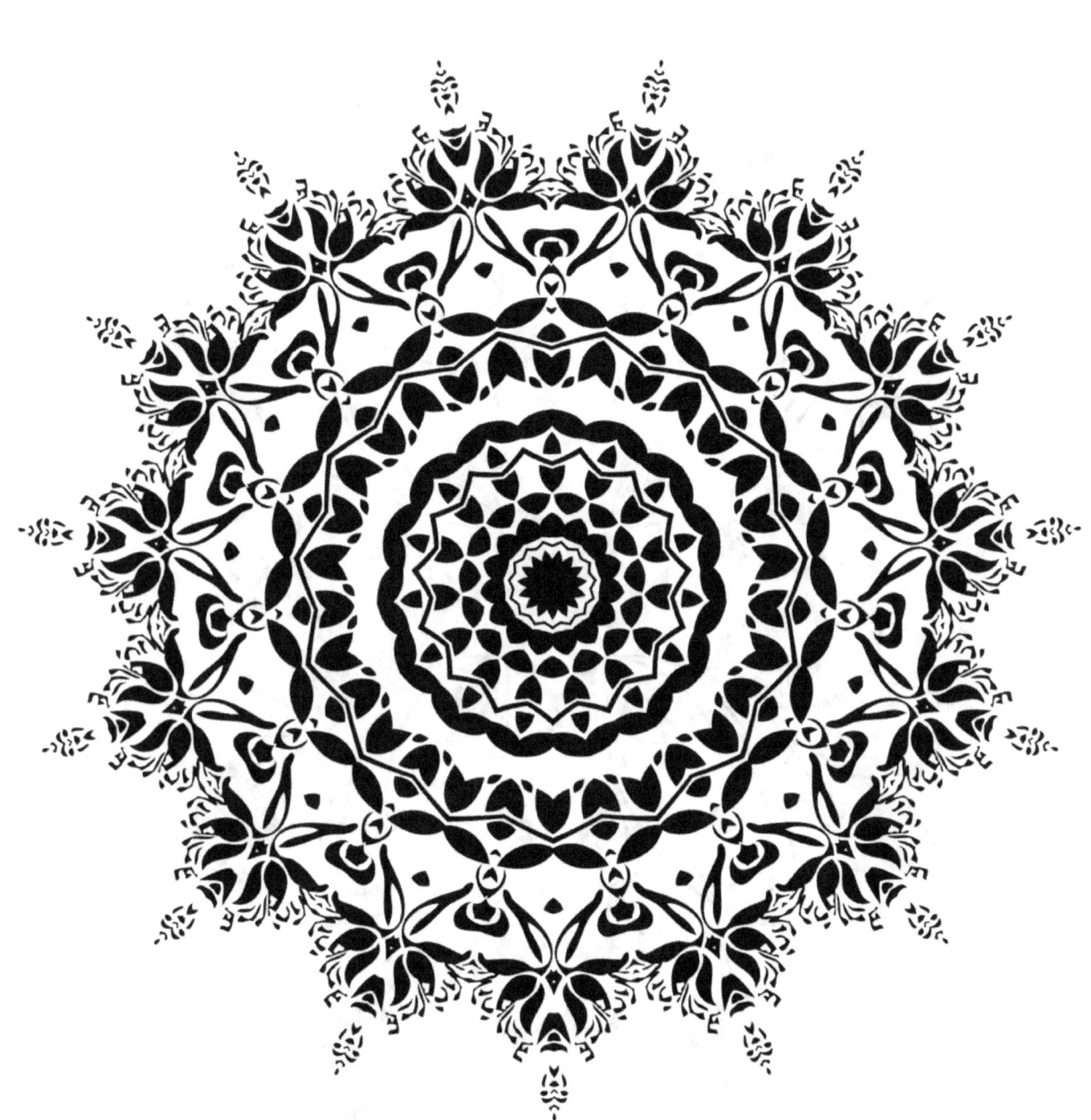

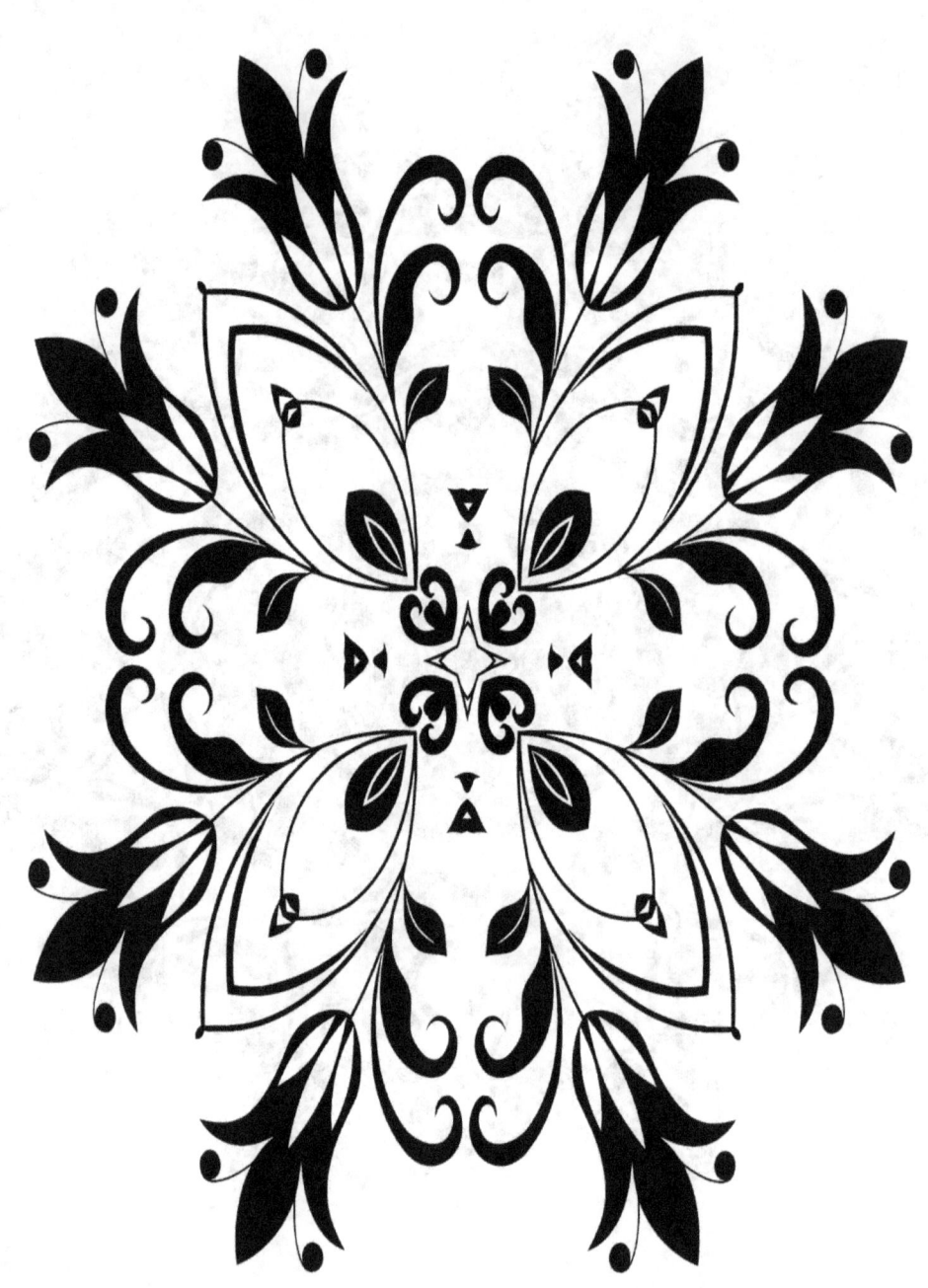

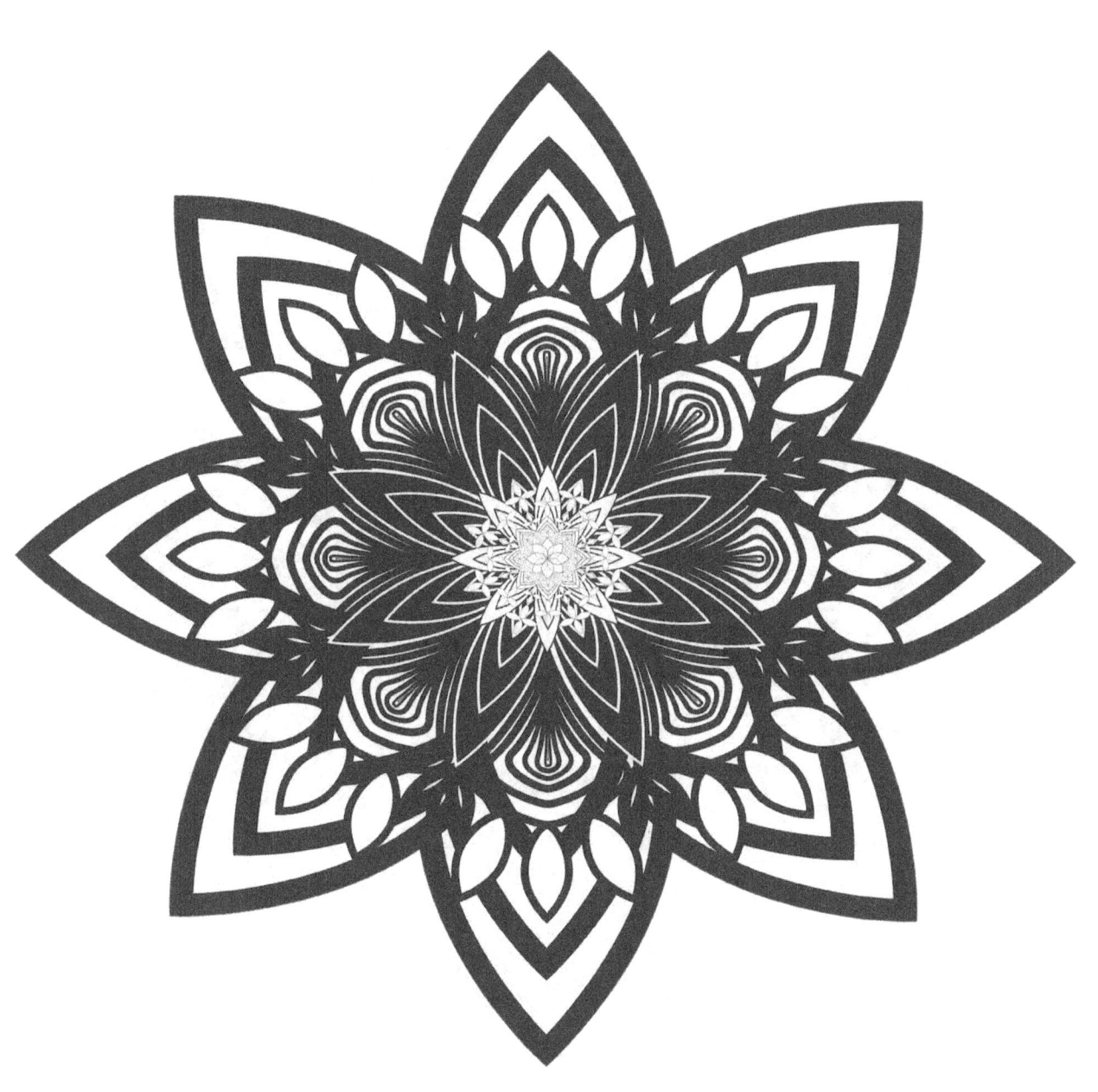

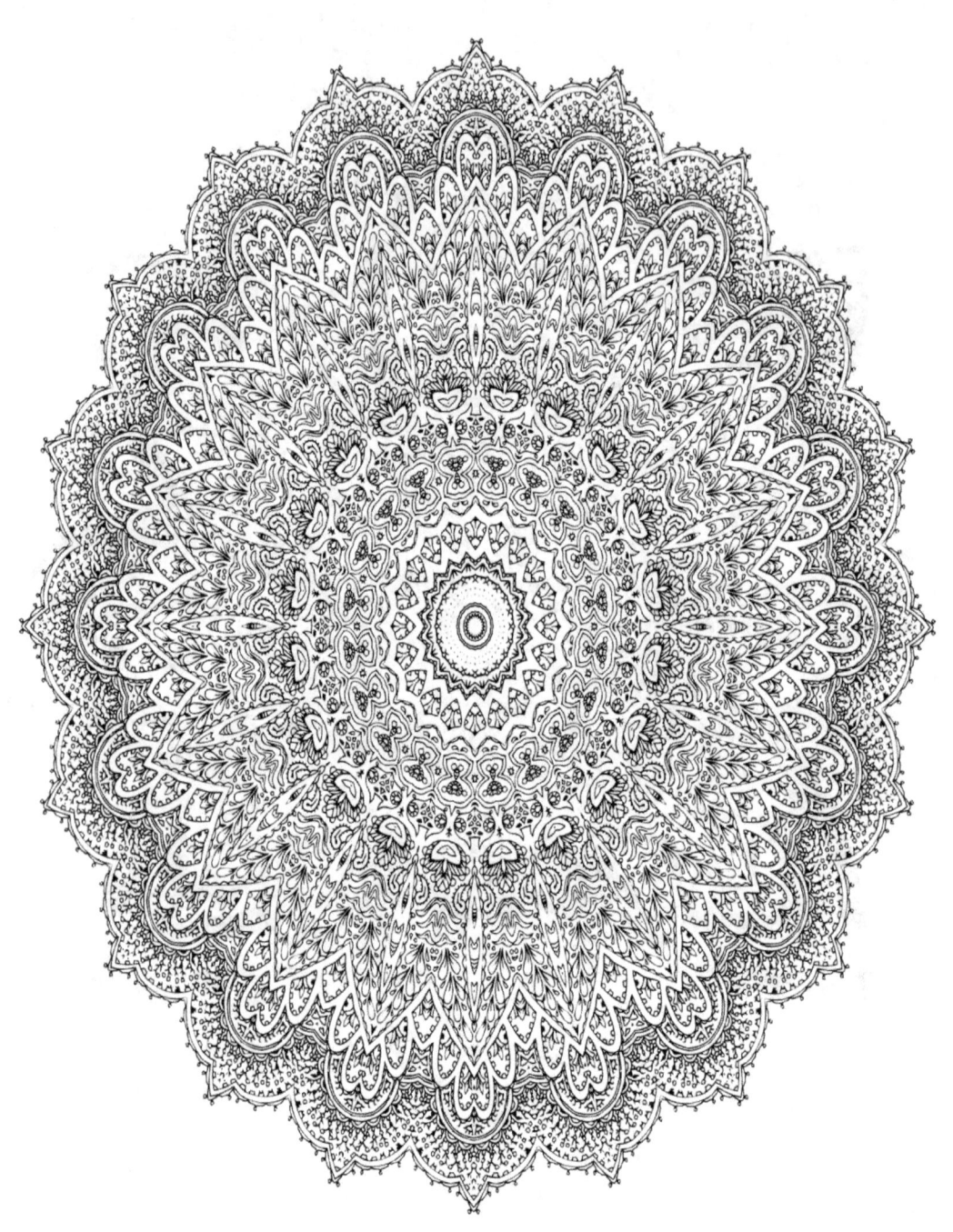

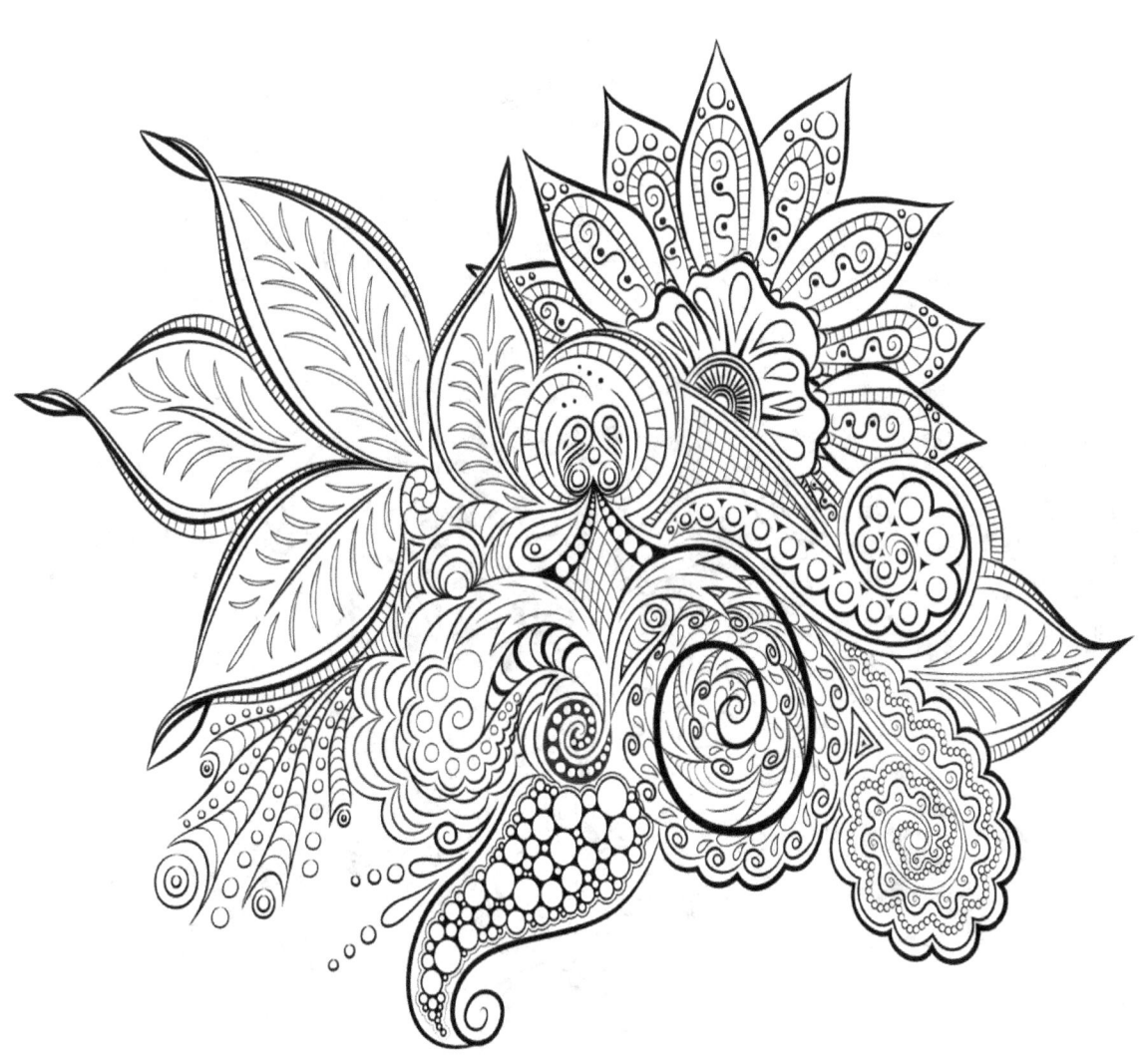

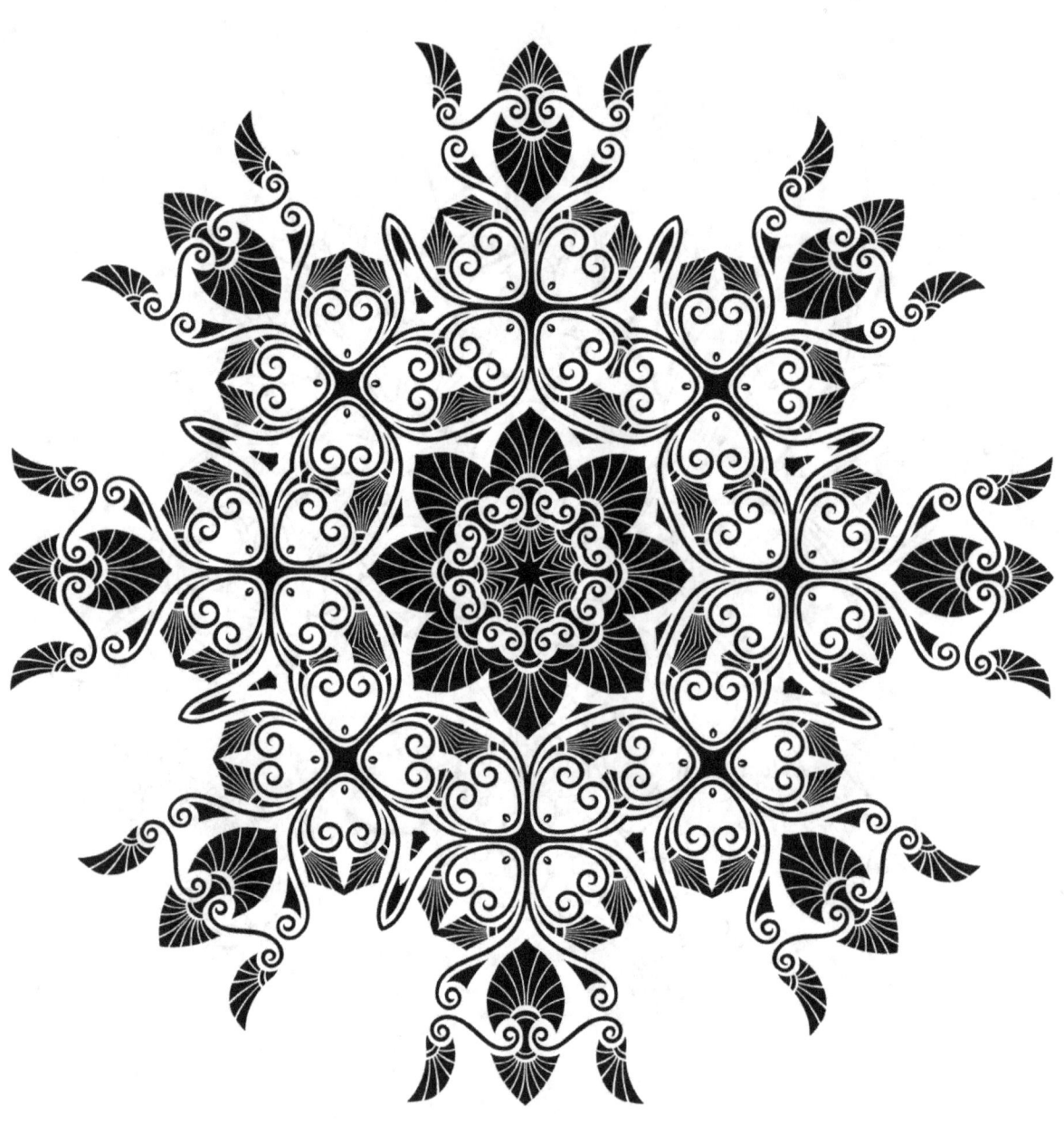

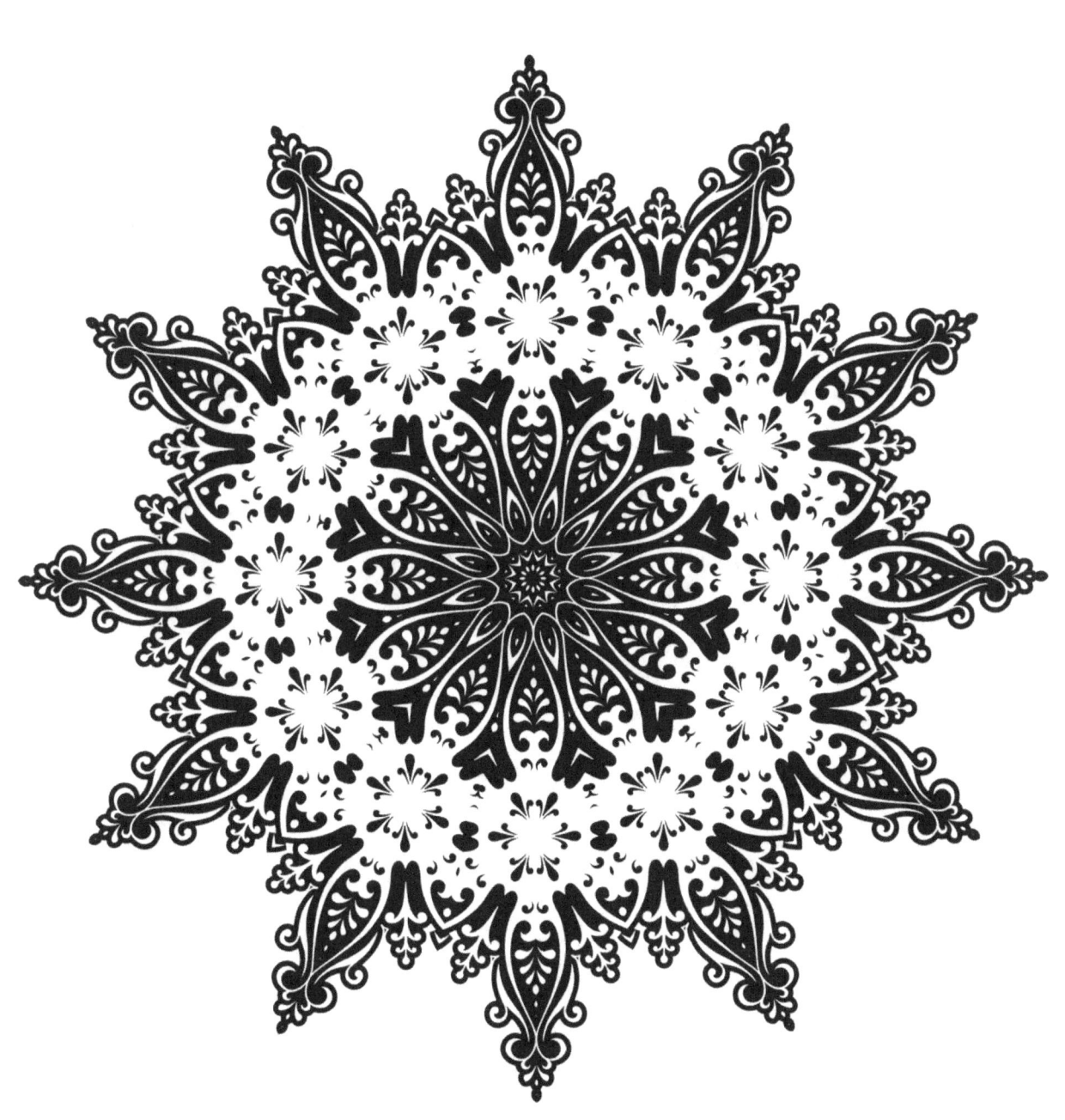

www.ingramcontent.com/pod-product-compliance
Lightning Source LLC
Chambersburg PA
CBHW080556220526

45466CB00010B/3163

WE TRAIN TECHNICIANS

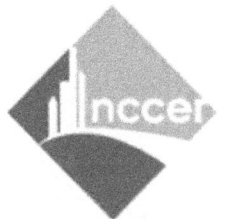
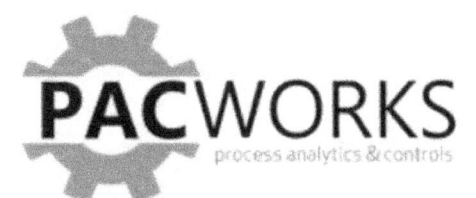
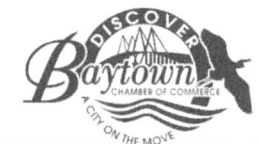

PAC Works
219 Defee St.
Baytown, TX

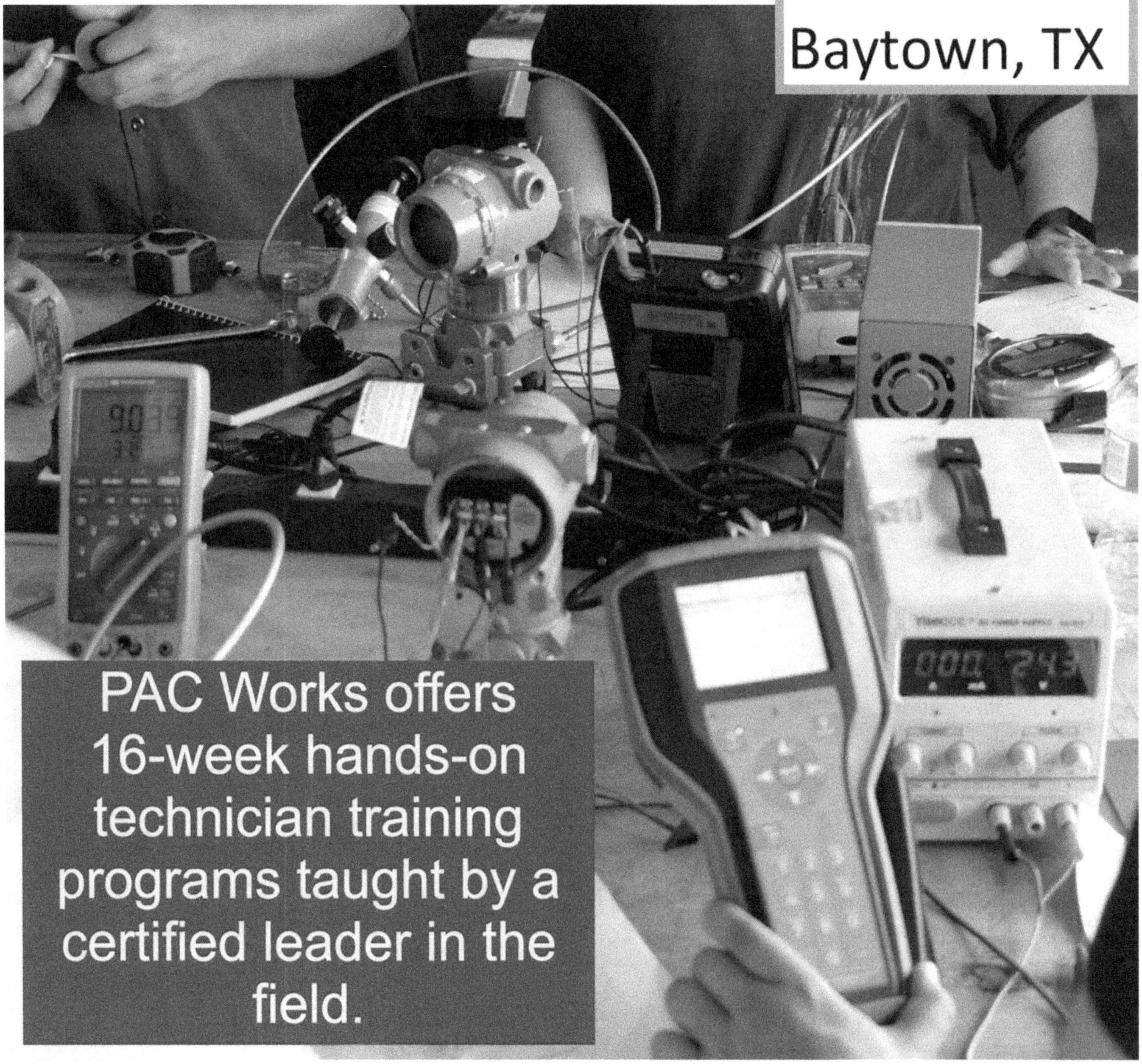

PAC Works offers 16-week hands-on technician training programs taught by a certified leader in the field.

Call Us | (832) 926-4717